I CALL BULLSHIT

I CALL BULLSHIT

LIVE YOUR LIFE, NOT SOMEONE ELSE'S

JOSHUA MILLER

LIONCREST
PUBLISHING

I CALL BULLSHIT
Live Your Life, Not Someone Else's

ISBN 978-1-61961-869-5 *Hardcover*
     978-1-61961-870-1 *Paperback*
     978-1-61961-868-8 *Ebook*

For my beautiful and amazing wife, Cynthia, thank you for holding me to a higher standard each and every day, never letting me play a small game. Thank you for reminding me that anything is possible when love is present. I love you.

To my mom, who has never given up on me even when it would have been an easy option. You simply amaze me every day with your strength, love, and brilliance. Thank you for raising me with the moral compass necessary to achieve anything in this world.

To my brother, Jason, thank you for always being there and catching me when I fell in life. The laughs we share will bond us for life. Thank you.

In memory of my father, Charles, who never took shit from anyone. You would be proud of the man I have become. Thank you for showing me what living self-expressed means.

CONTENTS

The only thing **standing** between **you** and **your goals** is the **bullshit** story you **keep telling yourself**.

DISCLAIMER

The good news is, you just took the first step toward taking back your life by buying this book. The bad news is, you are full of shit.

I know, I just insulted you and it's only the first sentence, but wait—let me explain.

You see, we all are full of shit. You and me.

Scientifically speaking, we are all walking around with five to ten pounds of crap inside of us, but this isn't a diet book and I'm not here to tell you how to eat. I'm here to discuss a different type of shit—the bullshit.

You know, the type that robs us of our happiness, energy, and free time. When the BS takes us from enjoying our lives, we begin to settle and that's when everything slowly goes downhill. We start settling in these moments and believe it's OK, normal, or better yet, that we deserved it for some reason.

Newsflash: It's not, and you deserve better.

These moments are what I call bullshit, and when you get enough of them strung together, it leads to a pretty safe and mediocre life.

You don't have to settle for this, and that's why I wrote this book. After coaching for twenty years, I can safely say every human being has to deal with these very BS moments.

Some people deal with these moments like they're nothing. They become so used to settling that it's as easy as breathing. Others are overcome by them, and it's like a shark is pulling them under water.

I wrote this book to strike a nerve and give you the insight and aha moment you need to take action. Calling BS is about full transparency and going for the core. You have to be willing to look under the surface and discover what's holding you back—not because you need to, but because you owe it to the person who's waiting there to be discovered.

We all settle at times, but that, too, is a choice and just one of many options. We have all taken the shortcut or path of least resistance in our lives, but where has that gotten us? Are you completely fulfilled living a life with zero regrets? If so, feel free to return this book now. If not, I invite you to read on and discover just where you may have had a BS moment.

This book is a combination of my thoughts, life experiences (based on my mistakes), a brain dump (as one editor so kindly described it), and an amalgamation of coaching, advice, direction, and support to give you what I can only hope is a spiritual colonoscopy that will uncover where you are unfulfilled, help you begin to think differently, and ultimately get rid of your BS.

I promise you a bullshit-free book.

I believe in a world where we spend so much time taking selfies that we don't ever actually ever look at ourselves. Most people can barely stand the sight of themselves in the mirror. Because real change starts with physically and figuratively looking at yourself and asking some powerful questions. You've mastered the selfie; it's time to master the self.

This book will challenge you to see yourself, both as you are now and as who you hope to become. To find out who that person is, you will be asked to think deeply about many things you do in your life. You'll be challenged to look at how you think, how you act, and how you present yourself to the world around you—and I mean the real world, not your online profile.

You don't necessarily have to read this book in order. In fact, I encourage you to jump to the sections that appeal most to you. You are the one taking control of your life, so do it in the way that works best for you. Just as I'm not going to tell you how to live your life, I'm also not going to tell you how to use this book. My approach isn't about drinking the Kool-Aid or kale juice (depending on your preference). This is my life, my lessons, my mistakes, my story for you.

There will be certain times I'll include a call to action regarding a certain topic. You'll notice the words **HOW TO START** in bold in a couple of spots—these are opportunities for you to really engage with the process. I hope you'll consider them.

If you're committed to being bigger and better, regardless of what your environment is or what your friends say, this book is for you. If you're the person who cries every day because you can't figure out why your life is the way it is, this book is for you. If you're looking for a quick fix, however, you're shit out of luck. This is

not that. It's not a magic pill and there is no quick fix. Change is going to take some work. At times, you're going to feel uncomfortable—don't be afraid, you'll live. But you must do the work. No one else is going to do it for you.

My own coach always says to me, "This is the show. There's not a dress rehearsal. This is it. Either get out on stage, or go sit in the audience."

I sat in the audience for a long time, angry because I thought I deserved more. The "more" came but not until later, after I had done the work. I'm going to help you get there, too, and I'm going to do it without psychobabble, without overpromising, and most importantly, without any bullshit.

It's never too late to start. Today is a new day. Now get after it.

Kind regards,

Joshua

INTRODUCTION

Drip, drip, drip.

Crap, I thought, hearing the beat of water seeping through the faucet under the sink. *Just what I need—another project.*

Part of me hoped the leak would magically stop on its own. Maybe if I ignored it, it would simply go away or get better. The saner side of me knew I needed to get off my ass and do something about it.

With a heavy sigh, I did what most responsible people do in this situation—pulled up YouTube on my computer and watched a few videos about fixing leaky faucets (after I struggled to find the right Wi-Fi setting).

Yeah, I don't have time for this, I thought.

A phone call and an hour later, the Roto-Rooter person arrived at my door. *Yes, the cavalry is here.* He looked under the sink, grabbed an Allen wrench, used it for about thirty seconds, and was done.

"What did you do?" I asked, shocked this hadn't turned into an outtake from any one of those mind-numbing, yet addictive-beyond-belief HGTV shows.

"A screw was loose," the plumber said flatly. "I tightened it."

Well, OK, then. "Fair enough," I said, more than a little embarrassed. I thanked him, accepted his kind offer to keep the tool should the problem arise again, and sent him on his way to the next utterly inept homeowner who's watched too many episodes of *MacGyver* and assumes most of life's problems can be solved with duct tape and YouTube.

After the plumber left with his eighty-five bucks for three minutes of work, I realized two things: one, maybe I am in the wrong profession; and more importantly, two, this story is the perfect example for what's wrong with the self-help field today.

We have gotten lazy, people. I mean like Mike Judge's cult classic *Idiocracy* lazy.

Everyone's looking for a quick fix, and no one wants to take the time to learn how to properly understand and attack the core of our problems. We can't see what's getting in our way, because we are squarely in it. We aren't willing to figure it out ourselves, so we reach out to the two people who knows us best—wait for it—Siri and Alexa. I know, I know—you thought I was going to say your loved ones or mom and dad, but nope, not even close. It seems with all the technology, our homes are getting smarter while we are slowly regressing.

The bottom line is, we want someone else to swoop in with an Allen wrench and stop the leak for us. But if we want to learn, to really change for the better, we must do the work ourselves.

If you don't, you're going to be standing in a puddle of disappointment.

If we don't get curious about what we do and why we do it, we are doomed to come up against the same emotional blind spots and challenges again and again, and that's the real danger. We settle.

Mediocracy becomes the norm, and we begin to build our lives around a bar that's been placed so low you could bump your head on it while sitting on the couch watching Netflix. We convince ourselves the lives we're living are as good as they're going to get, and basically, we give up.

Oh well, we think, *my life sucks. Guess it's just gonna suck forever!*

Guess what? It doesn't have to.

Such negative thinking—which we all succumb to each and every day—makes me furious. I'm sick and tired of seeing people settle, probably because it reminds me of how much I've settled in my life (more on my own adventures in mediocrity later). As renowned author and spiritual teacher Marianne Williamson says, "Our deepest fear is not that we are inadequate. Our deepest fear is that we are powerful beyond measure."

The I-guess-this-is-just-the-way-things-are mindset brainwashes you until your life becomes as mediocre as you believe it to be. That's not living. That's existing. If you have resorted to living a life that is anything other than the one you truly want to live, I call bullshit.

No one is immune to making these mistakes. I've had to call myself out on my own screw-ups. Often. Look, there is only one big difference between you and me: I've had the tough conversations and have been working on myself for a long time. I've looked in the dark places under my bed, befriended the bogeyman, and looked at my own life with Scully and Mulder *X-Files*-style curiosity and *Seinfeld*-like observations of the absurd. I know where the bodies are buried.

Everyone has one chapter in their life they don't talk about in public. This book is mine.

It's taken me almost twenty years to be OK with who I am. I don't want you to wait that long. I did the work and I'm a far better person, father, coach, brother, husband, and son for having done it.

I feel deeply that my personal experiences and my professional training have prepared me to help you become a better person as well. But before I tell you how you can change your own life, let me tell you a little about how I literally fell into the career that would alter the course of my life forever.

WHO IS THIS GUY TELLING ME HOW TO LIVE MY LIFE?

A disclaimer: I'm going to talk about myself for a couple of quick paragraphs. I hate talking about myself, but my editor thinks it will help you relate more to me. If you don't feel like you need to relate to me, by all means skip to the next section. If you want to know a little about a kid from Manhattan who learned a thing or two from his awesome parents and the city that raised him, all while trying to fit in and mostly failing at it, read on.

If you skip the rest of this section, here's what I really want you to know: I'm a guy who struggled to figure out who in the world he was and spent a lot of time learning from my own mistakes. I've been where you are, and I do not own a soapbox. I know what it's like to have no clue who you are or what you want out of life. I also know what it takes to figure that all out. I did it, and I'm going to use my experience to help you do it, too.

Much of who I am today, for better or worse, comes from my upbringing in the heart of NYC. I'm not talking about the city many know today. When I grew up, the Meatpacking District actually had meat, NOHO was simply called North of Houston, and Times Square was most certainly *not* a family destination. It wasn't all bad. In fact, I wouldn't have it any other way. It's all I know.

Despite going to a pretty high-profile private school, I wasn't a great student. I was a solid C+ performer, which in my school was considered shitty. I never thought of school as my best teacher. Life was my teacher. I learned from the city, from my experiences, and from watching others and figuring out how they saw the world. I was open to real experiences, and there was no place better to find them than NYC.

My favorite teacher, however, was hip-hop. I took in everything while listening to my mix tapes of Stretch Armstrong, Funkmaster Flex, and Kool DJ Red Alert. Some people had babysitters; I had these guys. Hip-hop spoke to me in a way nothing else did, and it still does. (Not what you expected from the guy in the photo on the back of this book, right?)

Of course, I also learned a lot from my parents. Here's the thing—I could write an entire book about my mom and dad. But here's all you really need to know: My parents raised me with a strong sense of morality. They taught me what love is. They also taught me to be independent and how to think for myself. My mom was the rock of the family, and my dad was the kind of guy who would be there for you no matter what. He was completely unabashed when it came to showing the people he loved how much he cared about them. Much of who I am today is because of the man he was.

Despite not loving high school, I did graduate (barely) and went to Syracuse to study in the unbelievably challenging communications and design program. With the incessant snow, the two full-time jobs I had to hold down, and the rigor of the curriculum, I was beyond stressed.

During my senior year, right in the middle of all of this stress, I got a phone call that would ultimately change the course of my life.

THE CALL THAT CHANGED EVERYTHING

On October 27, 1995, my family called to tell me my dad had cancer. They said it was treatable and everything would be fine. They lied. I knew it then but didn't want to admit it and neither did they. They also suggested I not come home for Thanksgiving and should possibly skip Christmas as well (insert alarm bells blaring in my head here). They didn't want me to panic, lose my focus, and drop out of school. Well, two out of three ain't bad. I panicked and my focus strayed liked a cat following a laser pointer, but I took their advice. I didn't get to see my father or my family much during my senior year. I set my sights on graduating.

When I finally did see him, my dad was a shell of the man I knew. I barely recognized him.

Doctors had given him just a few months to live, but he was able to miraculously hang on long enough to come and see me graduate. His presence there was the biggest miracle and best graduation gift I could ever ask for. Soon thereafter, his condition worsened. He was dying. I tried to start working, but I spent most of my time with him in the hospital by his bedside.

In December of that year, my father passed away, and my life would never be the same.

CALLING MY OWN BULLSHIT

The loss of my father devastated me and would change my life in ways I could not begin to understand and still struggle with today as I write this book. Everything I thought I knew changed in that moment. It took years for the enormity of the loss to sink in, during which time I basically poured myself into a soulless but lucrative career in the world of advertising, design, and marketing. I worked at some of the largest ad agencies and launched brand campaigns for *Fortune* 500 companies across the globe.

I had an excellent job. I was making mid-six figures. I was in my early twenties and living on my own in NYC. Life looked great from the outside. On the inside, I was miserable.

Losing my father at such an early age made me painfully aware of how fleeting life is. And yet, I was working eighty hours a week with zero work-life balance and less than zero happiness. I was hanging out with people who cared more about hanging out than actually doing anything with their lives. I knew I wasn't living the life I wanted and that I needed a change, but I wasn't sure what to do or how to do it.

HOW I LITERALLY FELL INTO COACHING

One day, I was leaving my office in Midtown on a Friday

evening. As I walked into the chaos and the swarm of humanity buzzed all around me, someone bumped into me, and I took a nosedive onto the sidewalk. Literally.

I sat up in a haze as legs swished by me and used the cold and unforgiving city cement as a cushion for my ass. Blood gushed from my nose. I couldn't even register what had just happened, let alone get myself up and out of the way. In typical New York fashion, people just kept walking by me. I'm surprised no one took my wallet.

Finally, a woman stopped and asked if I was OK. I said, "I'm not sure." I was far from home, and I didn't know where the nearest hospital was. I probably had a mild concussion if I was willing to talk to a complete stranger. She called an ambulance and was kind enough to wait with me until it arrived, which again, in typical New York fashion, took so long I could easily have searched WebMD, self-diagnosed my injury, and headed to a Walgreens to patch myself up.

I opted to wait and am glad I did as all that time turned out to be the forty-two minutes that would change me forever. The woman and I started talking, and I learned she was an executive coach for a large consulting firm. I asked her, "What is it you do?"

"I help people," she said. "Basically, I make people happy."

"That's a thing?" I asked. The concept of "happy," and I mean *really happy*, was foreign to me at this point.

I asked again, "Is that a real job?" I hoped she took me seriously as I looked like I just went one round with Georges St.-Pierre. "I don't remember my high school career counselor telling me I could make a living making people happy. How do you do that?"

"I coach people," she answered in her cool, calm way. "I help people discover what's blocking them and then figure out ways to remove those obstacles so they can grow and learn and be happy."

It was too good to be true. My NYC cynicism, skepticism, and sarcasm all competed to speak at the same time leaving me speechless. Yet her words resonated deep within me. I felt something calling to me, and thankfully, it still wasn't the ambulance. I knew I needed to pursue this further.

I didn't believe in accidents, and although this wasn't the Matt Damon movie, *The Adjustment Bureau*, something felt oddly right. We exchanged contact information and met for coffee the next day—me with gauze up my nose and tape around my black eyes. I wrote down everything she said, scribbling furiously on napkins. I wanted to know everything I could about what she did and how she got there.

I still have the napkins from that first coffee meeting. I keep them as a reminder of the moment that made me think honestly about what I wanted. It was because of that conversation that I earned my certification and became the coach I am today.

Of the eight million people who are in Manhattan on any given weekday, the one who stopped to help me in my time of need was the one who would set me on a path I never would have found on my own. You might call that fate or destiny. I call it the answer to questions I had been asking all my life.

FINDING ANSWERS

For years, I had looked at everybody else around me in envy. "Why can't I be like that?" I'd ask, or, "Why can't I have that?" The questions riddled me constantly and sometimes haunted me at night. I didn't just want to keep up with the Joneses—I wanted to crush them. The pressure I was putting on myself coupled with the intensity of living in New York had given me an "eat or be eaten" attitude, but it wasn't who I really wanted to be.

These kinds of conversations we have with ourselves are debilitating to our psyche, to our emotions, and to our ability to connect with people and ourselves. And yet the answer is so simple: You can have anything you want. It's all about priorities, passion, purpose, and commitment. Living any other way is complete bullshit. Figuring out how to is the real journey.

My father once told me, "You'll never know what you can do until you try." One day, after he died, I was eating Chinese food and opened a fortune printed with those exact words. I've carried that fortune in my wallet for twenty years as a reminder. I am living proof that you can have your cake and eat it, too. You can eat a couple of slices of cake. You just have to figure out what kind of cake you want and how you're going to get it.

LEARN FROM MY SUCCESS (AND MY MANY MISTAKES)

Most coaches out there are "by the book"—in most cases, they're by their own book. These books are often filled with models, quadrants, and fancy terms and acronyms.

I'm not that coach and this is not that book.

I'm only interested in one question: how am I going to get you to recognize your own bullshit and squash it once and for all so you can go from where you are to where you want to be?

To answer that, I'm going to pull from every training

resource, schooling program, movie, joke, and quote I have in my arsenal. It's what I've done for the many clients I've had the privilege of helping throughout my career.

My approach has worked for twenty years, and I truly believe that when someone trusts you to come into their life with the expectation that you're going to make them happier, stronger, and better, you take that responsibility seriously and do everything you can to make it happen. We spend so much of our lives covering up who we really are and putting on fronts to impress people who don't really care about us at all. When someone is willing to drop the act and get real with me about becoming a better version of themselves, I take that extremely seriously because it tells me they are ready to open up and get to work. My only interest is getting you what you want so you can be happy and healthy.

I don't, however, believe self-improvement all has to be dry and dreadful—there's nothing wrong with injecting a little humor into the process when appropriate. Some of the most powerful influences in my life outside of my family are brilliant observers such as John Stewart, Dave Chappelle, John Oliver, George Carlin, Jimmy Fallon, Chris Rock, Larry David, and Jerry Seinfeld (to name just a few). They make us question the things we never would have otherwise. When it comes to calling bullshit, these guys are the best. I want to do the same for you, and if that takes a little irreverent humor at times, so be it.

I do believe that we all deal with the same shit, no matter if we drive a McLaren, a Mercedes, or a Miata. Oh, let's not leave out those who do the driving for us. I've coached people all over the world, from all walks of life. My experience has taught me that whether you're an actor on the cover of *People* magazine or a struggling single parent working two jobs, you will need to deal with your own insecurities. Someone with money can probably push off dealing with them for a little longer than most, but no matter the size of our bank accounts, we're all human. We all breathe air, we all have blood, and we all have to deal with ourselves.

How I coach is how I wrote the book. I want to give you things to think about and appeal to you on an intellectual level, but more importantly, I want to give you information that resonates with your heart. That is where the work happens. It's easy to go back and forth from an intellectual standpoint, but if you want to reveal the truth, you must get to the heart of what's stopping you from finding happiness. In these pages, I will teach you how you can stop hiding from these things and finally shift them once and for all from a hindrance to a hopeful place.

PART I

SELF-HELP
NEEDS HELP

CHAPTER 1

GET READY FOR A CHANGE

Your legacy is being written by yourself. Make the right decisions.

—GARY VAYNERCHUK, CHAIRMAN OF VAYNERX,
CEO OF VAYNERMEDIA, FOUR-TIME *NEW
YORK TIMES* BEST-SELLING AUTHOR

There's a skyscraper in San Francisco called the Millennium Tower. It's fifty-eight stories high—the tallest residential building in the city. It was built in 2009, and by 2016, it was sinking.

Turns out, this particular building had some structural issues that caused it to start to tilt by one inch more every year, and now the developers are shocked that no one wants to live there. No kidding! It's the Leaning Tower of San Francisco. The foundation is obviously compromised. Who would want to live like that?

Yet if we look at how many of us live our lives, we already set up on faulty foundations. We slowly sink and tilt until we literally become hunched over in our old age. It's like spiritual scoliosis, and it slowly sets in over time without our even noticing.

You can change, but you must start with a solid foundation by reconnecting with your true, authentic self. You don't need to rip the entire house down, but you do have to do some work to make real changes, little by little.

For many years, I didn't put in the work. I thought I was working, but in reality, I was only putting my energy toward a life that was completely inauthentic. It was complete bullshit.

When I got into coaching, I realized there are no shortcuts. There's no quick way to find out who you are and what you want. If you truly want something more than the life you're living today, even if you don't yet know what that might be, it's going to take effort, time, and doing things you have never done before.

If you're reading this book, you're already taking steps to

improve. Something resonated with you—maybe you've even had your "bullshit moment" and finally admitted you are sick and tired of being sick and tired. You are not being true to your authentic self—you might not even know who that person is. **And if you continue to do nothing, I can make one guarantee: your life will stay exactly the same.**

If you have reached that point in your life, I want you to know:

- You are worth more.
- There is more.
- It's possible to get there.
- It's going to take work.
- There's not one scientifically proven way that's going to solve your problems.
- There are ways to help you get the process going.

There is hope, and the answers are within you. The process begins by looking at yourself. Figure out what your blind spots and bad habits are, then commit to creating something else.

The following are just a few things I hope you get out of this book. Each concept overviewed in the rest of this chapter will be explored and explained more fully in chapters to come.

WHAT BULLSHIT IS HOLDING YOU BACK?

If you're like most people, you've probably never stopped to ask yourself, "What's my purpose?" If you're like most people, you don't know what "purpose" even means. Many times, purpose is confused with passion (more on this topic in chapter four). When I ask my clients to tell me their purpose, they usually have a few questions of their own: "My purpose? Where? Here? Today? On the planet?" The answer is: yes, all of it. Think bigger than yourself. There is no right or wrong answer. To figure out what it means for you, look beyond your environment, your friends, your social media feeds. You must look inward.

Once you know your purpose, the work really begins. Now, it's time to figure out why you haven't fulfilled it yet. What's holding you back? Is it fear? Ego? The fear of your ego? That nasty voice inside your head telling you you'll never do the things you want to do? If it's any or all of those, good news! You're just like everyone else.

Knowing these two key pieces of information—what you should be doing and why you're not doing it—will start you on the path to becoming the person you want to be.

CULTIVATE YOUR OWN HAPPINESS

Happy people don't have the best of everything; they make the best of everything they have. If you don't act, you're not going to get anywhere. It's that simple. You have to physically do the work. We've gotten good as a society at expecting others to do the work for us, but self-improvement is one area where you can't just throw some money at it and make it go away. If you want to get your dream job, you can't hire someone to get it for you. If you want to find love, you are required to go on the dates. Don't expect anyone else to be responsible for your happiness.

When it comes to figuring out what you want out of life, there is no need to overcomplicate things. Simply ask yourself what truly makes you happy, and figure out how you're going to do it. What do you care about? What lights you up? The answer might be something you can do professionally; it might be something in your personal life. Either way, pinpoint what it is, start to think about how you can get more of it in your life, and then take steps toward it.

DON'T BELIEVE THE HYPE

When it comes to self-improvement guidance, it's far too easy to find information that says exactly what you want to hear. The stream of articles and advice is endless: Do This, Don't Do That; Top Ten Habits of Productive People (because, you know, productive people only ever do ten things); Work Hard, Not Smart; Work Smart, Not Hard; and on and on, forever and ever.

I've tried, read, and practiced all of these things, and I've found there are only a few fundamental things that really work. Strip away all the noise and focus on what's within you, not whatever is the fad of the moment. This book will help you do that by boiling down some of the basics effective in helping you figure out who you are, what you want, and how to get it. I am living proof of what works (and what doesn't), and I want you to benefit from my experiences—good, bad, and everything in between. Simple as that.

MAKE BETTER HABITS

All people have bad habits. I call them "emotional blind spots." You don't know what you don't know, and until someone holds that mirror up for you, you're bound to keep repeating the same behaviors.

I was talking to one of my friends on the phone one night when he told me he had a goal of running the New York City marathon. I started to tell him how cool I thought that was when I heard a clunk. "What was that?" I asked.

"Sorry," he said. "I'm making a martini, and I was just eating some dessert."

"Oh," I said. "What are you eating?"

"Double chocolate lava cake," he mumbled through a mouthful.

Wait a minute. "So you're having a martini," I said, "and a double chocolate lava cake. How often do you have that?"

"Every night," he said. "It's my ritual."

"You're committed to getting in shape to run a marathon, but your nightly ritual is a martini and a double chocolate lava cake?" I asked.

"Yeah," he said, followed by an awkward pause. "Is that bad?"

I can only hope he realized in between bites and sips that the way he's living his life is just a tad out of line with the life he claims to want to live.

We all do these things, and we usually don't even realize it. Jerry Seinfeld isn't the only one who has to deal with one-uppers, double dippers, and close talkers. We all do things that either keep us from our goals or push people away. Figure out what your bad habits are—easier said than done, I know, and we'll explore ways to make it less painful later—and form some new ones that work for you.

FIGURE OUT WHO YOU REALLY ARE

It's very likely that you don't feel like you're living as the person you truly want to be and that's probably because you're not. We all have been there, some longer than others. You may have reached a point where you feel as if changing is impossible. As E. E. Cummings said, "It takes courage to grow up and become who you really are."

We all set up our lives in ways that allow us to stay comfortable. As a result, we're never challenged to grow and learn. We become complacent, and instead of thriving, we just exist. In fact, we get skilled at just existing, and before we know it, we have no idea who we are or what we want. We wake up one day and think, *What the #@!&? This is not the life I wanted or hoped for.*

When we start to think those thoughts, many of us get pissed at the world and start playing the victim, blaming everyone and everything for how life got to be the way it is. Such a reaction—again—is normal but not a solution. It's nothing more than a temporary release at best.

Reconnecting with that person you want to be takes some serious digging around in those areas we don't want to discuss with anyone. Ignoring those areas is like deleting files on your computer—you think they're gone, but they're still there, just hidden in the background. They're the insecure nagging conversations you have all the time from that little annoying voice in your head, the same one that at this moment is asking, *Why did you buy this book? Will he stop talking and get to it already? Who is this guy, and why are you reading his book and not Tony Robbins's or something?*

To finally address these areas once and for all, you're going to ask yourself some powerful questions that you've never asked before. For example, what are you afraid to know? What's the one thing you least want to accept in your life? What can you sense without knowing? If you ask these questions and don't like the answers you get, that's OK and normal, but you still have choice. You can quiet the voices telling you you're not worth it and begin to work toward having a real, authentic life. I call making such a change Getting Rid of Your Bullshit.

When you can tune in and reconnect to your authentic self, things will change. People will show up in your life differently. Life itself will be more rewarding and rich. I know it sounds like overselling, but I've experienced it myself and I see it when working with other people. Make no mistake, it's going to take work—anyone who tells you otherwise is full of shit—but it can be done. Much more on this level of life-changing authenticity can be found in chapter three.

DON'T BE AFRAID

Are you scared? Or are you not ready? There is a difference.

If just reading what I want you to gain from this book already has you thinking, *Holy shit! I'm not ready for this!* Great. A visceral reaction to some of the aforementioned topics is a good thing. That means you've already stepped outside your comfort zone. Hang on and breathe. You ultimately get to say how your life goes, not me, not this book—you and only you. You don't have to swallow all the information in one huge gulp. Pace yourself. You will make these changes slowly, little by little. **Obstacles are just opportunities in disguise—as long as you choose to learn and grow from them.**

I know you can become the person you want to be. You can identify the limiting beliefs that have kept you back, deal with the fears and emotions that are getting in your way, eliminate negative thoughts and become a more positive thinker, and find increased meaning and satisfaction in your daily life.

WHY I'M CALLING BULLSHIT

You might deeply believe you're not worthy of a better life. You might think life dealt you a bad hand, and there's nothing to do but accept it.

That's bullshit.

Instead of living a life you've "accepted" or, worse, living a life you think others would want you to live, stop and ask yourself what you want. You got to the point you're at now because you made choices, some great and some shitty. It's OK. We have all done the same thing. At some point, you also decided to stop challenging yourself in some areas of your life and that's when you hit cruise control. Now is your opportunity to shift gears, to act in a way that will make you feel whole and happy.

Anybody can change. I love it when someone laughs at the idea of changing their life. It tells me that they are scared of something and that fear can be a great driving force to motivate you into action. Every second of every day, you have an opportunity to choose how your life is going to go. You and you only. You can always turn it around, because at the end of the day, life is a series of choices strung together. Those choices create a story—you're either going to tell your own or give the pen to someone else to write it. And because Morgan Freeman likely isn't available to narrate your life, you might as well start doing it yourself.

Change is possible, even if you're already hustling just to get by. If you've looked around your life and decided it's not the one for you, you've already taken a step so many others can't bring themselves to face. We have either stopped asking ourselves important questions, have been asking the wrong questions, or are asking the wrong people.

NOT ALL QUESTIONS ARE CREATED EQUAL

When something doesn't go right in your life, what do you do? If you're like most people, you get upset or frustrated. You might go for a few drinks. You might find someone to complain to. Maybe you go to the gym, or exercise, or change up your environment. These are all just ways to avoid the question, "What's really happening here?"

There is a significant difference between asking yourself "what" questions rather than "why" questions.

"Why" questions will typically lead you down an emotional path. If I ask you, "Why do you think your life is like this?" you're going to have an immediate, visceral reaction. The answer will likely end up bringing you down rather than building you up. However, if I ask you, "What do you think caused this?" it sparks a much broader, bigger conversation, which is the type of conversations you want to be a part of.

"WHAT" QUESTIONS TO ASK YOURSELF WHEN YOU HIT A DEAD END OR EXPERIENCE DISAPPOINTMENT:

What is the biggest obstacle that stands in your way right now?

What's the lesson here for you to learn?

What's your role in how this unfolded?

What will have this go differently next time?

For more thought-provoking questions to ask yourself, **see the appendix.**

You must let yourself be vulnerable when answering such questions. Humans hate showing weakness, but sometimes, that's what it takes to get to the real root of an issue. You might need to grieve. If you've lost a job or a loved one or some money or any of the other things in life you can lose, it's OK to be upset. In fact, it's critical to allow basic human emotion to take place. People and society tell us constantly that looking weak is not good. You won't get the girl, the job, or that "thing" if you are too expressive or emotional. Let's be clear: I'm not saying you should bare your soul to anyone who will listen. I'm saying that when you tap into the real you—the heart of the matter—people will listen and show up differently.

No one ever tells us how to express ourselves fully because the world condemns it so often, so we have no idea what to do once we have. I learned early on that expressing yourself comes at a cost. Sometimes, it's a hefty price. People don't always want to hear the truth about what you feel. I spent many (probably too many) years shutting myself down in fear of upsetting other people or looking weak. I have since stopped that, and it's been the most satisfying act I could ever take. It's taught me how to become responsible for who I am and to trust that I will deal with whatever comes my way. It took work, and it was worth it.

If you don't let yourself become vulnerable, you won't experience life the way it was intended. You're not going to be able to move forward because at some point, you will feel like you are somehow missing out and the perceived unfairness of it all will stop you in your tracks. Getting past this feeling is going to suck, and it's not going to come easily, but the more you do it, the less scary it will become and the more authentic a life you can have.

When you don't spend time learning from your mistakes, you're doomed to repeat them. It's why you've always had the same type of romantic relationship, the same type of boss, the same office space, the same career, the same challenges with money, or your body, or your brain. You're not learning, and you're doomed to keep living an inauthentic existence.

Everyone is entitled to take a breather when shit gets tough. For some, that breath comes in the form of yoga, while for others, it's a drink with a friend and great conversation. Whatever it is for you, do it, then remember to pick yourself up and start asking yourself some of the aforementioned questions (**check out the appendix** for more). That's going to move you from victim to victor. Lights out on your pity party; it's time to move on.

STOP ASKING THE WRONG PEOPLE

How many times have you found yourself in this situation where something doesn't go your way, and the first thing you do is call a friend to whine? They listen, then say something along the lines of, "Screw that," or, "That's their loss," or, "That was definitely not your fault." You feel better for a second, then you hang up. Then you wake up the next day, and you still feel like shit. Why?

You haven't done the work.

You think you did and it feels like some effort was exerted, but don't be fooled. It's the equivalent of reading life's *CliffsNotes* and faking your way through another day.

If you want real answers, just ask yourself what went wrong. Then take the time to dissect and learn. Yes, I know this sounds easy, but it's not. If it was, we would all be happy, fit, rich, in love, and I would be out of a job. If you don't, you're just inviting those bullshit thoughts back in: I'm not good enough. Why bother? There's no point. It's always been this way. Too often, we keep those thoughts in our head like a nonstop playlist—all day, every day. The only way to stop them is to figure out the truth behind them.

When you feel yourself getting down on about your life, I want you to think of Nick Vujicic. Nick was born with tetra-amelia syndrome, a rare disorder characterized by the absence of arms and legs. That hasn't stopped him from doing everything he's wanted to do: he's a painter, a swimmer, a skydiver, a dad, and a motivational speaker. There's absolutely no stopping him. He's a great example of mind over matter. He took what many would see as a life-ending disability and found his voice and purpose in motivating and inspiring others. As he said, "Often, people ask how I manage to be happy despite having no arms and no legs. The quick answer is that I have a choice. I can be angry about not having limbs, or I can be thankful that I have a purpose. I choose gratitude." Really think about his life, then tell me whether you still feel sorry for yourself.

GET OUT OF THE BULLSHIT RUT

If you're done with the bullshit, there are some ways you can start moving down the path that leads to your new life. You can prepare yourself to stop settling, then face and overcome your biggest obstacles. Along the way, you can eliminate negative thoughts and emotions, and you can break away from limitations.

STOP SETTLING

To start making real changes, you must first become aware of the fact that you are currently settling. Sorry, but it's true. Just take a look at the four main areas of your life—finances, relationships, career, and overall wellness—and do an audit of your life. Ask yourself, "Am I aware of what's happening? Am I doing anything about it? Where do I want to be in a year from now? Five years? Ten?" Your answers will become your goals. (More about how to explore these areas of your life will come in chapter two.)

Don't be afraid to dream big. Be afraid of not dreaming. As writer Anaïs Nin said, "If you limit yourself only to what seems possible or reasonable, you disconnect yourself from what you truly want, and all that is left is compromise."

You're going to come up with a million reasons why you shouldn't bother. It is so easy to give up before you even start. The path of least resistance is always the most appealing option, but consider where so many people would be had they taken it. Nasir Bin Olu Dara Jones, who most people know as Nas, grew up in the projects in New York, among relentless gang violence, drugs, and killings. He went on to become one of the greatest, most respected rappers in the hip-hop community today, and he did it by believing in himself, working hard, and going after the life he wanted. He could've given up so easily—all the evidence to support why his circumstances were bigger than his dreams were right in front of him. But he didn't give in to it and neither should you. Your desire just has to be bigger than your circumstances.

You need to believe there's more out there and that things can get better. If you don't feel you are worth having more, you won't create more. You'll only create enough to fill up the size of your current cup of life. I say make your cup bigger.

FACE AND OVERCOME YOUR BIGGEST OBSTACLES

To hone in on what's standing in your way, you may need to ask yourself if you have even tried moving forward. Many times, we confuse conversations with constant action, and they are just not the same. As we discussed, expressing yourself is good, but speaking to the wrong people or asking the wrong questions is not. It's like getting into a car with no destination. You'll drive around for a while, then eventually run out of gas and end up frustrated. **Your first step is to figure out the why.**

Ask yourself, "When was the last time I was genuinely happy?" Where were you? Who were you with, and what were you doing? It can be a difficult exercise for most people. If we were playing *Family Feud*, the top three most common responses would be, "I can't," "I don't remember," and "Why bother?"

If any of those are your answer, then I call bullshit.

Really put some thought into it. Remember a time and a place when you felt fulfilled. Where were you? Who were you with? What were you wearing? Doing so reminds you that happiness is possible, you experienced it before, and you can do it again.

Did I mention it's going to take some hustle on your part?

Once you know what makes you happy, find ways to have more of it in your life. Those who are truly happy know what it is that brings joy into their life and protect it at great lengths. They nurture it so it can grow and continue to be a source of what fuels them.

So what's that for you?

When you start to create a life that's more fulfilling, you stop settling for less. Period.

You realize you are worth having more. Why start sitting in coach if you can afford first class?

You're going to make some difficult choices along the way—some of the things that no longer fulfill you are going to have to go if you want to make room for more of what makes you happy. They may include friends, coworkers, lovers, partners, homes, jobs, and of course, all those nagging bullshit conversations you are constantly having.

It could be as simple as not picking up a phone call so you can stay present with a loved one or as complicated as leaving a job you hate. Just remember that where you focus your energy and your attention is where your actions will follow. If you believe life sucks and the status quo is the best it's going to be, that's the level of intentionality you will bring to your life. If you believe you're ready for and capable of change, you can have so much more. As author Brendon Burchard said, "Something extraordinary happens when you dramatically increase the focus, drive, and intention you bring to your life, work, and relationships."

Are you ready to go to work?

ELIMINATE NEGATIVE THOUGHTS AND EMOTIONS

You must become mindful and present to what you're allowing yourself to think and feel. Your brain is hardwired for certainty. When it doesn't have certainty, you start to make assumptions and jump to conclusions such as *I'm not good enough, I'm a fraud, she's never going to write me back, he's never going to talk to me.* Pay attention when those negative thoughts and feelings creep in. You can't address what you don't recognize.

Confronting these things can be tricky. We're intuitive beings—even the most unaware person still gets a blip on the radar when something happens that doesn't resonate with him or her. Some people just pay more attention to it than others. Your body is designed to protect you, and sometimes, that works to your detriment. At the quickest sign of anything that's going to potentially harm you, your body goes into flight-or-fight mode. But sometimes, the thing that scares you is the thing you should face head-on—that's how you break through.

HOW TO START: Slow down and listen to what's going on in your mind and body. Pay attention to those blips. They are there to help you, not hurt you. Drowning them out will only make them come back later, but this time, it won't be a little blip. It will be like nails on chalkboard grinding through your head.

Mindfulness and breathing exercises can help, but of course, you need to understand how to do them. For some people, yoga is a terrific way to listen to themselves. For others, it's painting, reading, writing, hiking, or any other number of activities. Switching up your environment also can help you see things in a new way. I am a big believer in shifting my environment and settings, every hour at least, to gain a new and fresh perspective.

Disconnecting from technology also can help enormously. Imagine if we unplugged and recharged ourselves as much as we do our phones. I know most people's social lives revolve around social media, but I've never met anybody whose world ended because they didn't log on to Facebook. In fact, there are studies linking depression with exposure to too much social media. You think you're looking at things you deserve or wish you could have, but most of it is not real. You're seeing only what the posters want you to see, and comparison is the thief of joy.

Getting to the heart of your negative thoughts and feelings requires being present. I know "mindfulness" and "meditation" have become ubiquitous buzzwords as we humans desperately attempt to detach from the insanely busy world we have worked so hard to create, but there is real value in being able to just sit quietly with your own thoughts. And despite what some other authors would have you believe, it doesn't cost a single cent to do it. Find a place where you can close your eyes. Last time I checked, most bathrooms have doors and locks on them.

If you truly can't find a place away from the rest of the world, stick cotton balls in your ears, drown out any outside noise, and simply be. See if you can sit there for five minutes. Start with one minute and work your way up. Just start. Listen to the thoughts in your mind that have been competing for your attention. Learn to silence them. The more you give yourself time to sit and think in silence, the easier it will become to shut those voices down when they decide to start screaming at you in your head.

WHAT ABOUT YOUR FRIENDS?

As I previously mentioned, many of us have our own bad habits, but sometimes it isn't about what is holding you back—it's who. We all surround ourselves with people who will allow us to remain comfortable with the status quo. These are the "friends" you commiserate with when you just want someone to agree with everything you say. They are the people who tell you your dreams are way out of reach. When you realize your purpose in life, everything around you should go toward fulfilling that purpose. If a person in your life is not supporting that, not pushing you forward, or is holding you down in any way, it might be time to cut him or her out entirely.

HOW TO START: Ruthlessly audit each of your friendships. Think about the moments when you might really need somebody. Is that person going to show up? Don't believe me? Call or text that person at 3:00 a.m. and see if they answer. If the answer is no, it may be time to think about whether you need them around. When you realize you need more in your life, you'll need to make sure the people around you are going to prop you up, not pull you down. The bigger game you play requires a better supporting cast. Think of it like a sports team: what if the same players formed the starting lineup at every game for ten years straight? Injury would inevitably set in and their ability to perform would suffer. If you aren't constantly putting people on the bench or cutting them from the team, burnout will take over.

Remember when I asked you to think about where you want to be in one, five, and ten years? Do the same thing again, but this time, also write out a list of all the people in your life. Ask yourself, "Are these the people who are going to help me achieve those goals?" If you have any doubt, cross them off the list. **There's a spot in the appendix where you can do this right now.**

Deciding who stays and who goes is not easy—in fact, it can be downright brutal—but trust me (or better yet, trust your future self), it's worth it. There is no joy in admitting you don't want someone around anymore. But in the end, you will be better off for surrounding yourself with the people who truly get who you are and what you are all about.

A DIFFERENT APPROACH

As you can likely tell by now, I'm not going to waste your time like so many self-help books out there. I'm not telling you what to do, nor am I reinventing the wheel. There's nothing new here—everything in this book has been said before.

The problem is the way it's been said. Look, I get it: the self-help field is packed with the best, new, different approaches and models on how to be better, get better, and do better, and that's a good thing.

The problem I have found is that too many people have taken these concepts and either overcomplicated them or twisted them into a marketing machine, ripping away anything of real value and oversaturating an already jam-packed industry. One day it's step back, the next it's lean in, then swerve out of the way. What's next? At some point, it's all become too complex, which is why I felt compelled to tell my own version of what you probably already know.

I am not Tony Robbins, Wayne Dyer, or Deepak Chopra, who have incredibly powerful and uplifting messages. In fact, without them, I wouldn't be here today.

The difference between me and them is that I am just a regular person like you who started living a life and at some point, realized I took a left when I should have gone right and have been working my way back ever since. What I learned is that going back is the wrong direction. The key is to keep moving forward. The natural tendency is to retreat, but don't. It will actually take you longer, only to realize you are fine right where you are.

I've been working on myself for twenty-plus years. Do I have all the answers? No. Do I have what I think could work? Yes, but no one can tell you whether it will work. Only you can do that. I'm not standing on a soapbox here. I just want to share with you what I know to be true, with the hope I can help you in some way connect with the person you want to be or the person you hoped that you would become.

In addition to my own experience, I have a long list of people who have inspired me in so many completely different ways, and without their influences, this book wouldn't have made it to fruition. It includes:

- Dwayne "The Rock" Johnson
- Sir Richard Branson
- Dave Chappelle
- Gary Vaynerchuk
- Seth Godin
- Lewis Howes
- Oprah Winfrey
- Judd Apatow

- Ellen DeGeneres
- Tony Robbins
- Jimmy Fallon
- Steve Weatherford
- Conan O'Brien
- Jim Carrey
- Nas
- Jim Kwik
- John Stewart
- Simon Sinek
- LeBron James

I can't thank them enough because without their knowing it, each of these people in their own indirect (and sometimes direct) way has inspired me to be the best version of myself and dig deep during times of doubt only to discover I had what I needed in me to move forward.

HOW YOU CAN USE THIS BOOK

I want you to find what resonates with you within these pages. Reread the sections that speak to you most; skip the ones that don't. When you read something that resonates with you, view it as a sign and do something with it. Don't toss it away or ignore it. If you read something and think, *Who is this guy telling me about my life?* I urge you to pause. **HOW TO START:** Breathe and check yourself for why you are reacting that way. It's a sign—don't ignore it. What did I trigger?

If you are compelled to turn to a specific chapter, identify one little action related to that topic and work on it. You can even write down what that action would require of you and come back to it later. This book is meant to be a guideline for you to do your own work, learn to think differently, and to do it in a way that makes a tangible difference in your life. These are the instructions—what you do with them is up to you.

Whatever you do, don't settle. That's where the bullshit creeps in, and once it does, cleaning it up can take a lifetime.

CHAPTER 2

LOOK IN THE MIRROR

Manifest in your dreams, wake up with intent, hit the ground with a purpose, but more than anything, execute with relentless desire.

—STEVE WEATHERFORD, SUPER BOWL CHAMPION, TEN-YEAR NFL VETERAN, FITTEST MAN IN THE NFL, SUPER DAD OF FIVE

As a society, we love a quick fix (even though that doesn't really exist). We want the magic pill (bad news: that doesn't exist either). We think all the answers to what we're seeking are just a Groupon offer away. Admit it: at the very least, you've been tempted to attempt to solve your problems with a few swipes of the phone. Maybe you were lying in bed thinking about your weight when a Groupon sale for a thirty-day juice cleanse appeared in your inbox. All you have to do is buy the deal, then send the coupon to a few friends and you'll be on your way to your goal weight. Easy, right? Wrong. This is the trap we have all succumb to. We take action but haven't actually really done anything. You've shelled out some money, sure, and hit Send a few times. You might even do that cleanse and shed a few pounds (maybe). **HOW TO START:** Ask yourself, does any of that result in long-term change? Have you made any real improvements? Are you any better off at all?

If you're doing a nod of shame right now, don't. We've all done it. There's so much out there thrown at us. Fads are shoved down our throats everywhere we turn. It makes sense to reach for your phone in a time of crisis. The problem is, it just won't make a difference.

Instead of chasing that quick fix or magic pill (did I mention those don't exist?), it's time to ask yourself some questions.

QUESTION 1: I'VE BEEN WORKING ON MYSELF FOR A WHILE. WHY ISN'T ANYTHING WORKING?

Maybe you have a deep-down desire, even a need, to be better. This need compels you to cling to the newest, most buzzed-about fad of the moment out there. You gravitate to it. You read the book, you go to the seminar, you do the workshops. *This will work!* you tell yourself. You are pumped. Then you go back to your day to day and feel utterly unchanged and unfulfilled.

Here's why: When you're in that moment of learning something new, your endorphins are running. You convince yourself that this time, this thing will work. It's like playing lotto—as the number rises, you believe your chances of winning are greater, so you play and tell yourself, *This is it. It's my time.* The author or instructor has given you just enough—a hit of good energy and encouragement. Then, time's up. If you want more, you must sign up for the next course. As soon as you leave that workshop, or you shut that podcast off, or you finish that book, reality sets in. Life shows back up. And you find yourself no better equipped to deal with all of it than you were before.

The entire self-improvement industry is just made up of ideas. Sometimes, they're great ideas. Sometimes, they're esoteric. Sometimes, they're made-up, ridiculous nonsense. Whatever they are, these ideas are not always easily presented in a way that encourages real action. We struggle to apply them. You might decide you want to become more successful, so you read articles titled "The 10 Qualities All Successful People Have in Common," or "The 7 Principles to Master Success in Life." When you're done, you expect to be better equipped to become a titan of business or the next mega-rich mogul. You won't be.

Those kinds of articles and lists are nothing more than instant gratification. They require nothing of you, so you do nothing, and you remain exactly the same—someone who yearns for success but who does nothing to go get it. Books, workshops, and seminars with the same confusing information are just as dangerous.

Yet, your tendency to be drawn to such stuff isn't really your fault. Marketing folks working in the self-help arena know how to reel you in. Most of what they're selling is driven by your very own ego and fear. Having worked in advertising and marketing for many years, I understand the psychology around how you appeal to people. When it comes to the marketing of self-help, there are two main approaches:

1. The Curiosity of More: Maybe there's more to life. Maybe there's something better. These are the ideas that conquer a person's tendency to stay anchored down. People never stay in relationships or jobs, because they are stuck in the mentality of improvement. The same thing applies to the people who stay anchored. They think there is nothing better out there for them. It's a messed-up paradox. The self-help industry knows there are enlightened people out there who have realized, *Hey, I could have more; I'm worth more.* Those are the people they market to.

2. The Nonbelievers: Then there are people who don't

believe in "better" necessarily. They have given up and resigned. The self-help industry works hard to reach out to these people, too. It sucks them in with, "Don't believe? Well, here's a book that will make you."

Regardless of how they get you, whatever they're selling doesn't matter when it's not something you can actually use to become a better person.

DECOMPLEXIFICATION: YES, THAT'S A REAL WORD

The self-help industry has become overly complex (understatement of the year alert). While it helps to have terms for things, self-help continuously revamps old language to make it seem new to the general public. It's what they use to reel people in, when in reality we are fed the same information over and over (and over and over) again.

At the end of the day, self-help has always been about you. It's about your habits, your mindset, your productivity, your time management, and your wellness. But we humans love to make things more complicated than they have to be, and the self-help industry knows that.

It reminds me of the time I was working with an executive vice-president who told me he was frustrated with his team because anytime he'd call a meeting, the conference room's whiteboard marker and eraser would be missing.

He decided to ask his team to come up with a solution. The next time he addressed the issue, his team presented him with in-depth presentations and blueprints and models. He was absolutely floored by the complexity and detail his team had gone—and not in a good way. It was ridiculous how much time they'd spent on what should've been an easy fix. He said to his team, "Has anybody considered going to Staples, getting some Velcro and a string, and just putting the marker and the eraser on the board so it doesn't go anywhere?" The answer, sadly, was no.

We have a natural tendency to overengineer things when, most times, the answers are so simple. **You've got to be able to see the forest through the trees. We're conditioned to focus on individual blades of grass.**

Overcomplicating things can be dangerous in the self-help world where analysis paralysis runs rampant. You end up staying inside the little world where you feel good and safe. Or you can lose yourself in the idea of self-help. There can be a sudden loss of identity. You start to speak the language of the information you take in, rather than applying the information and developing your own language.

That's what you've had going against you. Now, let me tell you why this time really will be different.

QUESTION 2: SO IS ALL OF THIS JUST A BUNCH OF BS?

You may be wondering why I—the author of this very self-help book—am slamming the industry that allows me to feed my children. I am not. In fact, if it wasn't for this industry, I'd probably still be working at an advertising agency and aimlessly wandering through life.

Am I any different than the people peddling other stuff? In many ways, no. But in the most important way, yes. Because I've been where you are. I've hit the point of *Seriously, this is my life?* I decided I was going to do something about it. I can tell you what works because I've done it all and come out on the other end happier, healthier, and just loving life again. Was it easy? Absolutely not. Was it worth it? Absolutely.

I want to help you do the same but without any of the smoking mirrors, overselling, and overpromising you may have come to expect. I want you to be able to walk away from my book and take action immediately.

Simply put, I think people deserve the truth, and here it is: you can have more, if you're willing to take the time to really dig in and get your hands dirty.

- **It requires commitment and a shift in your belief.**
- **It takes time.**

- **It's not going to happen overnight.**
- **You can have the mentality of "deserving" something.**

No one will ever hand you what you believe you deserve, particularly if it's something you haven't worked for; your own self-improvement is no exception.

You just have to get past all the hype to what's real—dig in, and figure some stuff out on your own.

REMEMBER: YOU HAVE A CHOICE

When I went to my first self-help seminar back in 1999, it wasn't because I wanted to go. Others pushed me to, basically by saying, "You've got to get your life in order. You're a miserable person."

This seminar had it all: perpetually smiling people, rooms as stale as two-week-old bread, no windows, a brisk chill in the air, and horrible seats cushioned with what could only be described as three Q-tips, leaving your lower back in pain for days.

I was that guy in the back of the room with a permanent scowl and that look of "Don't come near me; I'll bite you." I was that resigned and that arrogant. Then, the last moment of that last day, something just opened up and I began to feel vulnerable. I hated it.

It's like you're sitting there and all of a sudden, you recognize your shoe is untied. You don't know how long it's been untied, but you recognize that it's a danger, and you're going to have to do something about it. I sat there for three days with my "shoe untied." As soon as I noticed it, it was like a shock to my system, and I did not like it.

When my mom picked me up, she asked, "So what did you get from it?" I looked her straight in the eye, confused as to what I actually felt. Seconds later, I summed up how much it sucked and compared it to a cult. I did swallow back my ego for a moment and say, "In life, we have choices, and everything you do is a choice and then it's your reaction in relationship to that choice."

She asked, "And?"

"And what?"

She pushed, "What does that mean for you?"

Frustrated, I responded, "You just asked me what I got. I'm telling you what I got. Now you're asking me what that means for me? I don't know."

That story is a pivotal story for me, because I fought tooth and nail, but had I not gone to that seminar, I would have never realized I actually had a choice. As do you. You have a choice to say yes. You have a choice to say no, or you can choose to do nothing, which people often forget is a choice, just a disempowering one.

In life, we will all have these moments where our shoes are untied, or we're invited to go to some "seminar" or do something that's going to push us outside of our comfort zone. The natural tendency is to protect ourselves and say no. I invite you to take a hard look before you say no, because some people never get the invitation to begin with. If you get the invitation, you should take it. You can show up and be resigned, but at least show up because you're never going to know. Regret doesn't look good on anyone.

Doing nothing is a recipe for having more of what you already have.

But before you can decide to do anything, you must stop and ask yourself, "What do I want?"

QUESTION 3: WHAT ON EARTH DO I WANT?

If you've gone the self-help route and didn't have a great experience, it doesn't mean it won't or can't work. Instead, you need to take time to reset and ask yourself what you wanted to get out of that. **HOW TO START:** Ask yourself, did you know what you wanted? Were you clear?

You must understand what you want to get out of something before you go into it. You wouldn't go to a car dealership and buy the first car you see or go to a restaurant and order before looking at a menu. You'd do your homework first and figure out what you want. Today, no one evens accepts a date with someone without knowing their entire life story beforehand. You must apply that same curiosity toward your self-help journey. Don't be afraid to get a second opinion on things, and don't be afraid to do your research. If it takes a little longer, be patient—it's worth it.

Sometimes we need to be shocked a little bit. We need to remember where we started so we can recognize how far we've come. I remember going to a workshop where the coach asked me what I wanted to get out of the whole thing. My answers couldn't have been more shallow and materialistic. Everyone else gave answers that had nothing to do with themselves. I felt like I had zero sense of moral decency. I sat with that feeling for an entire day. Fast forward to a year later after I had done some serious work figuring out who I was and what I wanted. I rewatched that video and could not believe the transformation I saw in myself (thankfully).

The question "What do you want?" is loaded and powerful when asked in the right context. It's one we tend to not spend that much time thinking about. We're so busy making a living that we forget to make a life. Then we think we're not worthy or capable of anything else.

Whatever it takes, you have to get to the root of why you're doing something before you do it. Really examine what's motivating you, and make sure it's in line with your goals. Otherwise, you can skip the seminar—you've already failed before you even found your name tag.

You have to know want you want; you can't let life figure it out for you. A good place to start is looking at what I call the four categories of your life.

THE FOUR CATEGORIES

Over the course of my career, I've learned that no matter how much money you make, where you live, or what your title or status is, we all face challenges in four areas of our lives: finances, relationships, career, and overall wellness (meaning body, mind, and spirit).

FINANCES

Whether you have money or not, it can be a source of huge stress. Before you scoff, just look at how many people come into money and find it to be incredibly overwhelming. More than 90 percent of lottery winners go into debt within a year. The reason they make poor financial choices is the same reason we all do: no one teaches us about money.

I knew next to nothing about saving money until I read *Rich Dad, Poor Dad* by Robert Kiyosaki and basically learned I was doing it all wrong. Not knowing about finances can lead to a lot of self-doubt, which can give that voice in your head—the one telling you all the time that you're not good enough and you'll never be happy—lots to work with. We all struggle, but getting a handle on what you want your finances to be doing for you, whether you're scraping by or just hit it big, can make a world of difference.

RELATIONSHIPS

When I talk about relationships, I mean everything from how you interact with other people to how you treat yourself. Because honestly, one has everything to do with the other. Many times, the things we can't stand in other people are the things we can't stand in ourselves. People are just a reflection of us, and man, do we hate that.

Think about when you see someone walk into a room who seems confident, happy, and self-assured. What's your first thought? Chances are, it's something along the lines of, "I hate that person," or, "Ugh, look at them." It doesn't matter if you know them or not; your instinct is to loathe them. Their confidence reminds you of your low self-esteem, and it raises questions you're too scared to answer.

Until you tackle all the things you don't like about yourself, it's really hard to have successful relationships with other people. Relationships are tricky business, and we're going to talk about them a lot more in chapter eight, which is literally called "Relationships: With Self and Others."

CAREER

Have you ever asked yourself, *Why do I always have the same shitty job?* I'll tell you why right now: because you've never stopped to actually find a real answer to that question.

The first step is to get OK with the fact that you're going to have to have some not-so-fun conversations within yourself. I've never met anybody who is like, "Hey, I'm so excited! I'm going to go spend the next ten minutes thinking about why my career sucks and I can't get promoted!" Nobody talks like that. We live in a world where status is everything and so much importance is placed on what we do and where we do it. Whether you have a J-O-B, a career, or are a serial entrepreneur, you are spending half your day (if not more) working, and that falls under "career."

OVERALL WELLNESS

Wellness is a term that has grown in popularity over the past decade. There are many definitions out there, but the one I love the most is this: wellness is the state of being in good health, with a focus on your lifestyle, especially as an actively pursued goal. Your body is yours to take care of—emotionally, physically, and mentally—and it's the only one you get while being on this planet. Wellness is a commitment to something bigger than yourself and about creating good habits and routines around the different areas of your well-being to ensure you are taking care of yourself.

Now that you understand the four main areas of your life to focus on, here are some questions to ask yourself:

- What's important to you at the moment—that you could focus on today or even over the next twelve months?
- What's working well for you at the moment?
- What isn't working well at the moment?
- What have you done so far to improve things?
- What's the excuse that you have always used for not achieving your goals?
- What aspects of your life will be impacted by not reaching these goals?
- What is the biggest obstacle that you are facing, and are you willing to endure to see your goal become a reality?

- Where might you be sabotaging yourself?
- What are you going to do in the next twenty-four hours?
- How committed are you to reaching this goal?
- On a scale of one to ten, how motivated are you to achieving this goal?
- Whom do you need to speak to about this goal?

IT'S NOT YOU, IT'S EVERYONE

If you're reading all of this and thinking, *This is going to be too hard for me. Everyone else in the world seems to have their shit together. I'm the screw-up. Everyone else has everything all figured out*, allow me to assure you that that is 100 percent false. We all deal with this stuff, we all mess up, and we all are faced with a choice of how we want to go about getting our lives back in order. As motivational speaker T. Harv Eker once said, "If you are insecure, guess what? The rest of the world is too. Do not overestimate the competition and underestimate yourself. You are better than you think."

A publicist once reached out to me with a request to meet with her client, a pretty well- known Hollywood actor. After reading and signing a twenty-five-page nondisclosure security document, I met him. Within five minutes, a megastar who I'd seen on the big screen more times than I could remember broke down and cried in front of me. Here was somebody I was a huge fan of, someone I'd put on a pedestal for as long as I could remember, and he was experiencing the same fear and self-doubt every other human being deals with all the time. I was shocked in the moment, but upon leaving, I realized we're all incredibly similar and, of course, human.

Somewhere down the line, the perception that people must have it all together became what's accepted. Social media doesn't help. As soon as you accept the fact that such a perception is in no way based on reality, you can open up to yourself and do the work that will help you move forward.

It's time to take a good, hard look in the mirror. No, seriously—go take a look. I'll wait.

QUESTION 4: WHAT'S LOOKING IN THE MIRROR GOING TO DO FOR ME?

I'm a huge proponent of an old-school selfie. What's that? Just stare in the mirror. You don't need a filter.

No one does this anymore. We can't even stand to see our own reflections while we brush our teeth. Sometimes, it's because we don't like the way we look. Sometimes, it's because we are afraid of what it will make us start to think about. So what do we typically do? We stop. We look at ourselves and then we turn away. We don't want to look at it. It's uncomfortable.

Looking at your own reflection in a mirror forces you to see what's going on within. It gives you a moment to reflect. You will see something, and you may like it or you may not. The question is, how long can you be with yourself? Most people cannot sit in silence. They cannot be with their own thoughts. Some people don't even know what their own thoughts sound like.

When I first did an exercise of sitting in silence, I fought it tooth and nail. Every fiber in my body wanted to scream, jump up, and laugh. When you're able to look at yourself in the mirror, you're starting to create a level of intimacy and vulnerability with yourself. Once you establish that, you can then use your newfound understanding of intimacy and vulnerability to connect with another human being. And no, that doesn't mean invite someone to stare at a mirror with you.

You're not just staring at yourself like some self-indulgent narcissist. You're actually doing work that will help you get the things in life you really want.

HERE ARE SOME QUESTIONS TO THINK ABOUT AS YOU LOOK IN THE MIRROR:

When was the last time you tried something new?

What life lesson are you willing to learn today?

What do you love about what you're doing at work?

Do you celebrate the things that you have?

What things make you lose track of time?

When was the last time you were happy?

When was the last time you loved somebody else?

What makes you smile?

What's important enough for you to go to war over?

Which is worse, failing or never going after what you want?

When was the last time you listened to your own breath?

What's something you can do or you know how to do differently than most people?

Where do you find inspiration?

What impact do you want to leave on the world?

There's an old expression that says, stand for something or fall for anything. Most of us fall, and more often than not, it's because we're not clear on what our worth is. We're not clear on what we're playing for.

The act of looking at yourself and asking yourself a question or saying, "Hey, what am I worth? What am I playing for? What's my day going to look like today?" can be incredibly powerful, because it sets the tone for your mindset. If you tell yourself, "Today is going to be an amazing day," that doesn't automatically guarantee it's going to be amazing. It means that's the intention you set for yourself. It's up to you to make something amazing happen throughout the day.

Every day when I wake up, part of my morning ritual is setting a standard for what I want my day to be. **HOW TO START:** Ask, "How am I going to go about my day? Everything I bring to the day, no matter what happens, I'm bringing intentionally. I'm going to be intentional with my time, my patience, and my presence." There is something incredibly powerful about that versus waking up and saying, "Crap! I'm going to be late to work!" What will you bring to the rest of your day? Write it down.

Changing your mindset takes time and work. It's not as if you'll look in the mirror one morning and suddenly everything will change. It's not going to be easy, and it's not going to be quick. Do not expect the quick fix—that's bullshit. But if you put in the time and energy, you will start to find answers to questions you never thought to ask.

WHO HAS TIME FOR ALL THIS?

Answer: You do. If you don't believe you can take on another task, ask yourself are all the "things" taking up your time making you happy? Are all those things serving a greater good, a greater purpose? Are they bringing you closer to your goals, or are they just stuff?

We all have stuff. We all have errands to run. We all have to-dos. When you're constantly coming from a place of "I have to get this done or else," there's the implication of an impending consequence. That's not an empowering place to come from.

People have a twisted relationship with time. So many tell me, "Take your motivational mantras and inspirational quotes and go somewhere else with that. I don't have time for that." I get that, trust me. But we all get the same twenty-four hours in a day. The question simply becomes, what do you want to do with yours?

Everybody talks about time like there's not enough of it. Time really only matters when it's running out. When you're running late, when someone you love is sick, when someone is dying—all of a sudden, time takes on a whole new meaning.

After my father had gone through a couple of rounds of chemo and radiation, he looked like a completely different person. He wasn't the big gentleman, the big role model, the big dad I knew; he was this frail, skinny, pale guy. But all I wanted to do was be next to him. I wanted to hear his breathing. I wanted to spend every second I could absorbing his energy, because I knew it wasn't going to last. That's when time really matters.

We think we are immortal in our twenties and thirties, but as we get older, we start to realize that is not the case. None of us can afford to waste time, and effectively avoiding doing so begins with our relationships with ourselves. The conversations we have with ourselves either help us maximize our time or take away from it.

QUESTION 5: OK, I'M READY TO START MAKING A CHANGE. WHAT SHOULD I DO?

Set an intention for the day and don't be afraid to share those intentions with others to keep yourself accountable. If you tell people, there's a better chance those people will say, "Hey, did you make it? Did you do that thing? Were you successful?" Immediately, your level of accountability and awareness will be heightened. Your intentionality will soar.

I write my intentions down in three different spots. Perhaps you can put yours on your bathroom mirror or front door. The important part is to be able to visually intake your intentions as often as possible. Over time, your intentions will become reflex.

Plus, get crazy with it if you want. Have fun! When I first started setting intentions, I screamed them from the rafters: "My day is all about love and peace!" People thought I was crazy, but if it works, it works. I remember I had a client who decided to quit his cushy job and travel around the world (he is still traveling as I write this book). Everywhere he travels, he finds one word to inspire him from that destination and tattoos that word on his arm. It's all about personal preference.

HOW TO START: At the end of the day, before you go to bed, write down what you learned, what you're grateful for, and what you got out of your experiences. Keep a gratitude journal—**there is space in the appendix to get you started**. When you start to take on a sense of gratitude, it ignites a flame within. It creates purpose and makes you want more. Gratitude is critical for success and happiness. The best part? Anybody can do it.

Some believe wholeheartedly the key to their success has come from being grateful. Asking questions, looking in the mirror, taking moments of silence, unplugging from technology, and setting intentions will make a difference in your life. In the end, you get to say how your life's going to go.

This is not a time to come down on yourself—strictly force yourself to be nice to yourself. This time is about the things you accomplished.

Ask, what's one thing you'd like to be acknowledged for? Did you create value? If so, what will you take away? Was there anything missing, or are you incomplete? Give yourself permission to praise yourself and lift yourself up. Be grateful for what you're given and use it to propel yourself forward. Change your conversation of self-doubt into one of worth. When you start to do this day in and day out, the negative conversation will quiet. The cynicism and resignation of the world we live in will become less depressive. You will believe there's another way things can be.

CHAPTER 3

AUTHENTICITY: BACK TO BASICS

One of the most important things you can accomplish is just being yourself.

—DWAYNE "THE ROCK" JOHNSON, FAMED
ACTOR, PRODUCER, PRO WRESTLER, AND
THE "HARDEST WORKER IN THE ROOM"

Authenticity confuses people. Most assume it means being a brutally honest know-it-all or an arrogant jerk. It's really about being true to your own personality, spirit, or character.

Granted, you have to know what all those things are before you can be authentic about them. Sometimes, that means looking at the ugly, messy, nasty sides of yourself.

You know, the "stuff" we work so hard day in and day out to cover up, hide, and avoid talking about. When I say, "Be authentic," I'm telling you to find a way to stop being inauthentic.

Confused yet? Let's start with an example of one of the most authentic people I've ever known.

THE DOORMAN

Growing up in New York, I was exposed to every possible walk of life, ethnicity, and experience. The building where I grew up had a doorman named Frank. He was from South America, and he had ten children. For about forty years, I never saw this guy with anything other than a smile on his face. Even as a kid, I was always impressed with the fact that Frank chose to show up and be gracious and kind day after day after day.

Of the four hundred people living in the building, I don't know how many actually knew Frank had so many kids, or that he sent money back to Colombia to his family every month, or that he went to school at night to get his master's degree. But everyone knew from his smile that Frank was happy.

Frank's perpetual happiness caused me to continuously ask myself, "When was the last time you smiled about something?"

There were people who looked down on Frank, assuming he was "just a doorman," but he was so much more than that. He was an entrepreneur who owned a few businesses. He was a father, a husband, a student, and most importantly, a man who had worked for and appreciated the life he had. He chose to be a doorman because he knew it would help him make connections. He had passion, purpose, character, and spirit.

That's authenticity.

SO ONE MORE TIME: WHAT DOES AUTHENTICITY *REALLY* MEAN?

You, as a person, are authentic. If you go searching for authenticity, you're doing it wrong. Being authentic is just who you are. If that confuses you, take a look at the definition again: it's being true to your own personality, spirit, and character.

Authenticity is about striking a nerve to cause a big enough insight or aha moment. Too often, people take a prick to their nerve rather than a stab. They don't allow for full transparency.

Authenticity starts when you set an intention to be genuine, but before you can even do that, you must have an awareness of what a genuine intention looks and feels like.

Think of a race car driver—his focus never wavers while he's flying around that track. He intends to win that race, and he's going to do everything in his power to do it. Once you find that intentionality—which you'll remember from the previous chapter—the urgency to act in accordance with it will help you recognize your true, authentic self.

When you tap into your authentic self, your life will shift in a more positive direction. Your self-awareness will grow. Decisions will become easier. There will be more freedom around the choices you make, and you will remember what is important to you. Don't believe me? Have you tried? Ask yourself:

- Do you lie to yourself about what really matters to you?
- Do you compare yourself to others and come up lacking?
- Do you run on empty in order to impress others?
- Do you pretend to have a picture-perfect life?
- Do you hold back when you are not sure of the next steps?
- Do you need brand-name clothes and shiny cars to prove your worth?
- Do you spend your time proving to family or your culture you are worthy?

We all have the ability to choose how to live and uncover our internal blocks to personal freedom. These questions will force you to examine your life and think about any habits or people that may be stopping you from having the life you deserve. As author Jodi Picoult said, "When you're different, sometimes you don't see the millions of people who accept you for what you are. All you notice is the person who doesn't."

There are so many benefits to being authentic, too many to list, but my favorite is this: When you like you, others will like you, too. When you're in tune with you, you automatically—yet nonverbally—give those around you permission to get to know and like the real you as well. By doing this, you also weed out the people who may not be the best influences while attracting the right friends.

It can take a lot of energy to get there, but when you do, it's awesome. When you're being authentic and true to yourself, a lot of the internal noise and conversation that people jabber about (i.e., he said/she said; my ego this/that) will quiet, and you'll be able to live a more concise and passion-filled life.

Authenticity is about being able to stand in the presence of your imperfections. We are not perfect—none of us. The happiest, most successful people I've ever met as a coach are the ones who are happy with their imperfections. They embrace them. I'm not saying they love them, but they're willing to acknowledge them and understand how they make them who they are.

To be authentic, you must accept your humanity, embrace your talents and abilities, and be mindful that the process won't always be easy. You're going to be up against some unpopular people and decisions.

WHO WILL HELP YOU GET THERE?

Tapping into your authentic self requires you to seriously think about the people who surround you. Do they believe in your initiative to be authentic? If you're lit up about something and you want to pursue it because it feels true to your character, spirit, and personality, you can't let others take that away from you. If the people around you are willing to rain on your happiness, then you need to take a step back from them—maybe for the short term but maybe for the long term. (Remember back in chapter one when I talked about ruthlessly editing the list of people in your life? This might be a good time to reread that part.)

If you're worried about losing friends and relationships by being authentic, don't be. Another perk of authenticity is you begin to attract the right people into your life. The bad ones may walk out the door, but the good ones are still in the room or right around the corner, waiting to embrace you. Happiness begets happiness. People want to be around that.

It's also important to remember that as human beings, we're all on separate journeys. Many times, people will have an aha moment and immediately want to shove their miracle juju down others' throats. Yes, you will have a natural tendency to want to share with people how you've changed your life for the better, but proceed with caution. Otherwise, it can come off as exceedingly arrogant. When you're being authentic, recognize everyone around you is on different paths.

Be happy to share if someone asks, but don't force it on others. They need to have their own journeys.

Owning your life and being authentic is a process of taking full stock of what is and what isn't working in your life. Once you can do that, you can rely on yourself to be happy, not others.

LIVING AUTHENTICALLY MEANS LESS REGRET

If that's not an incentive to start being your true self as soon as possible, I don't know what is. We all have regrets, and most of them stem from the inauthentic ways we opt to live our lives.

Being authentic means being able to speak your mind. That means improving your argument, not raising your voice.

HOW TO START: Right now, I want you to close your eyes and think back to a time you didn't say what you wanted to say because you feared upsetting the other person or looking stupid. Ask yourself:

- How did that make you feel?
- What, if anything, are you still holding on to from that situation or exchange?
- How has that experience impacted your ability to be happy now?

Maybe you had a good idea for your boss, but you were too afraid to be shot down. Maybe you didn't tell someone you loved them because you didn't want to appear "weak." Whatever the circumstance was, I want you to ask yourself, truly what's the worst thing that could have happened? By holding back your inner self, you're being inauthentic.

Another common regret many of us share are the times we should have been the bigger person. It's something we all struggle with. Learning from such situations can be a lesson in hindsight, insight, and foresight.

- **Hindsight** is understanding a situation after it happens.

- **Foresight** is being able to predict what's going to happen.
- **Insight** is having the capacity to gain a deeper intuitive understanding of a person or thing.

Becoming the bigger person in a situation means being able to tap into all three.

Let's say you have a fight with a good friend. You both disagree on a political topic. Perhaps one of you is much more conservative than the other. You butt heads, and because you can't get each other to switch sides on the proposed topic, you throw out some nasty words to shut them down. Hindsight will show you guilt, but your ego might get in the way. You don't want to apologize, because you feel like you're giving in to their opinion. However, foresight shows you that if one of you doesn't apologize, your friendship may be frayed forever. So you must use insight and decide. Ask, what does your authentic self want from the situation? Push past your anger and ego, and gain a deeper, more intuitive understanding of why your friend stands on the opposite side.

It's OK to agree or disagree, and it's OK to be the first one to apologize. It doesn't make you weak, especially if it's done to save a relationship that means more to you than the argument.

There are many other ways living an authentic life can

help you avoid the regrets so many of us live with all the time. Now that you get what authenticity is and the benefits it can bring, let's talk about how you can get more of it in your life.

LIVING TRUTHFULLY

To find out you if you are living truthfully, you have to ask yourself some confronting questions. They'll force you to tap into your own intuition and push you past your comfort zone.

Take a deep breath, and get ready to do some serious digging into the places of your heart and mind that might not be your favorite spots to visit. It's OK if any of these make you squirm—just remember, if you want to be authentic, to be free, and have ease and joy in your life, you must ask yourself these questions.

ARE YOU HAPPY WITH THE VERSION OF YOU THAT'S SHOWING UP IN YOUR LIFE TODAY?

We all have different versions of ourselves that we present to the world. We all wear different hats for the different roles we play in life. We are sons or daughters, we're parents, we're caretakers, we're partners—the list goes on and on. Each of these roles requires us to make choices and brings with it a wide range of experiences. Those choices and experiences are strung together to tell a story—the story of you. **HOW TO START:** Ask, are you the starring role in your own story? What version of you is showing up in your life? Is it the version you are the happiest with?

IS YOUR PERCEPTION OF YOURSELF LINING UP WITH HOW THE WORLD SEES YOU?

Most of us are really good at pointing stuff out in other people (that person's overweight; that person eats with their mouth open; this person smells; this person doesn't know how to keep a secret). What about you? Are you 100 percent OK with how you look? Have you ever told a lie? When was the last time you showered?

So is the version of you that you think you're putting out into the world a reality? Or are you so busy finding flaws in others that you can't see anything wrong with how you're operating? If you think you are the wisest, kindest, most fun person around, who would agree with you? Has anyone ever called out a behavior in you that you chose to ignore (because in your mind, they were the one with the real problem)? Are there a lot of people who have a beef with you? If you can't figure out the root of the problem, just look at the common denominator. Chances are, it's you.

HOW IS YOUR AUTHENTICITY SERVING YOU?

Look at the four quadrants of your life that we outlined previously: finances, relationships, career, and overall wellness. The areas where you are not authentically showing up are likely the ones with the most problems. But the work doesn't end once you recognize the problem—you have to own it. Here is what you need to do.

HOW TO START: Take a look at your life. Right now, are you in a place where you feel loved by people? Do you have a job that lights you up, or are you one of those people who looks for every reason to take long lunches and bitch and moan? Do you find yourself taking the longest route possible to your j-o-b? Are you someone who is excited about the possibility of your future? Do you have love in your life? Do you want love in your life? Are you healthy, mind, body, and spirit, or are you winded by just getting to your car?

I've been asking myself these questions since 1999. I'm not going to lie to you. Sometimes, I cannot be with the question, and I surely cannot be with the answers, but I keep coming back and asking the questions.

Look at where you currently struggle in the four categories: finances, career, relationships, and wellness. Think about what this struggle is costing you in terms of happiness, sleep, and impact on others who maybe don't get to spend time with you or are confused by your actions. How are you not being authentic in that situation? What is the reality you're not facing in that situation? What don't you want to admit about the current struggle you're dealing with?

The answers may be painful to come to terms with, but they're answers nonetheless.

THE MYTH OF PERFECTION

As you look at all these components of your life, you're likely going to start to feel seriously bummed that everything isn't sunshine and roses. If you're like many people, the idea of being anything less than perfect is going to drive you up a wall. Here's the good news: perfection doesn't really exist.

We humans have made up the concept of what perfect looks like, and in most cases, they are spur-of-the-moment, unplanned, and unrepeatable flashes of time. Think about the last time you had the "perfect" moment. Have you ever had that exact moment again in the exact way? No. No matter how hard you want to, you can't go back to the same place, wear the same outfit, hang out with the same person, eat the same food at the same restaurant, tell the same jokes, have the same haircut—it will not be the same.

Once you accept the fact that "perfection" is not something that can be manufactured, you are free to stop chasing it. You can engage more fully in life as it comes and be ready to enjoy those moments when everything aligns, appreciate them for that they are, and move on.

AUTHENTICITY IS MESSY

I've said it before, but it bears repeating: getting to an authentic place in your life will not be quick, easy, or even all that fun. At some point, you'll have to become comfortable with the uncomfortable. The path to success or happiness, however that may look for you, will inevitably be messy. There will be times when you'll feel like you have zero control (because you don't—sorry).

Just like being perfect is a myth, so is the concept of control. You don't control things. You have influence, and that's different. Influence is a bigger, better concept.

There are things in life you can influence, and everything else is gravity—things you can't change. You can influence things by being actively engaged in life, physically, mentally, and emotionally. Dale Carnegie's *How to Win Friends and Influence People* has some great advice, including don't criticize, condemn, or complain; give honest and sincere appreciation; become genuinely interested in other people; and many other ways you can influence the world around you. I suggest you check it out.

By now, you should have a somewhat decent handle on who you are, who you want to be, and those are probably two very different people. Let's work on getting them more in line with some hands-on tools and techniques.

PART II

HELP YOURSELF: TOOLS AND TECHNIQUES

CHAPTER 4

HOW THE WHY BECOMES THE HOW

Achievement happens when we pursue and attain what we want. Success comes when we are in clear pursuit of why we want it.

—SIMON SINEK, OPTIMIST, AUTHOR, MOTIVATIONAL SPEAKER, AND FOUNDER OF START WITH WHY

We humans love to fixate on two things: the what and the how. What do you want to do and how are you going to get there? We love to think about the things we want. Maybe you want to be rich and successful. Maybe you want to be married. Maybe you just want to not hate waking up and going to work every day.

When we think about what we want, the next logical thing to consider is how we can get it. But before we can ever come up with a plan with the slightest chance of working, we need to know one more thing: why we want all that stuff to begin with.

THE WHY

When you jump in without figuring out the why, the how becomes an incredibly frustrating process. You must find the passion behind your what to have an easier and more successful how. Otherwise, there will be no sense of fulfillment or purpose. You'll just keep on being the person who simply clocks in and clocks out—basically, a glorified drone.

Earlier in my career when I was working in advertising, this is exactly what happened to me. My work life was just that—work. Eventually, I knew I needed a change. I had to do something. I thought about what I was best at and how I loved helping others, especially when it comes to discovering the best version of themselves. That's when I found my why. From there, I was able to figure out how I was going to best be able to help people, and I pursued a much more fulfilling and satisfying path in coaching.

The problem is, most people don't dig deep enough. They just scratch the surface. They never find what truly inspires them, and they tap out of life before it even begins. As Will Smith once famously said, many of us tend to just "spend money that we do not have on things we do not need to impress people who do not care."

People get stuck on what they want and don't focus on why they want it. Why is it even important? Why are you spending time thinking or talking about it?

One of the most depressing things I can remember about living in New York was riding the subway and overhearing people talk about their dreams or goals, then quickly hearing one of their friends shut it down by saying something like, "That will never happen. Why bother?" And just like that, it was Dream: 0, Unfulfilled Life: 1.

When you ask yourself why you want something, put some effort into the answer. "Because I do" does not count. That's a bullshit answer, and you know it. If that's your answer, you're being inauthentic. You need to challenge yourself more—don't be afraid of the conversation that might unfold. Ask yourself, "How badly do I want it?" A year from now, will I be OK if I don't achieve it? Will I be thinking about it five minutes from now? How about five hours? Can I picture myself achieving it? Really close your eyes and visualize it—what do you see? You will better yourself in the grand scheme of things if you have a reason for the success you aim to pursue. **HOW TO START:** If you can't get to the bottom of it, then ask yourself three variations of the same question: the first response will be automatic, the second will be what you think is right, and the third will come from someplace deeper. When you reach that deeper space, you're there. You just have to grab hold of it.

Acknowledge what you find, and let it guide your actions as you come closer and closer to getting what you want.

Part of the process involves having people around you who want to challenge you as much as you want to challenge yourself. The bullshit moment occurs when we let ourselves and the people around us slip into the same old conversations and enable our fears rather than champion our goals. We bitch, we moan, we complain, we commiserate, and at the end of the day, we are all the same miserable, stuck people we were when we started.

We keep on existing as life passes us by. Don't settle for existing—live.

HOW TO FIND THE WHY

Finding your why will give you the courage to be your authentic self. To do so, you must examine yourself down to your core.

First, be present with yourself. Unplug from technology. I can hear you gasping; trust me, you won't die if you miss a few tweets. Our reliance on technology as a distraction is astounding. In 2010, humanity consumed 1.2 zettabytes of information. FYI, a zettabyte is equivalent to about 250 billion DVDs' worth of info.

Ten years ago, we amassed that much in a year. Our brains are bombarded, and so we're on autopilot. We don't check in on our thoughts, because they're moving at the speed of light. We're a product of our environment, and our environment is chaotic, which is why it's so important to take a break every now and then and examine yourself for what you are without all the bullshit and distractions. Step away from your phones, people.

Once you do, you'll find yourself with some free time, and great news! You get to choose what to do with this time, whether it's reading, going for a walk or run, meditating, whatever. Make sure the activity you choose allows you to be completely without your internal conversation. In other words, get out of your own way.

We all have a unique gift to offer—take this time to discover what yours is. Think about your life and how it's contributing (or not) to the reality you want to have. Maybe you're hanging out with the wrong crowd. Maybe you have the wrong job. Maybe you live in the wrong place. None of that means you're not good enough or don't have the ability to be great. It just means you need to take stock, look at what makes you unique, and ask yourself what you can do to turn your "wrongs" into "rights."

Your why is inside you, waiting for you to discover it, and there are a couple of ways you can coax it out. Here are just a few ways to get started:

- Make a list of all the things that you love to do. Don't let money or time constraints stop you from writing anything down—let your creativity run free. Seriously, go nuts. Nothing is off limits here. Even if the thing you love seems crazy, it can offer insight into what really lights you up and makes you come alive.
- Ask your friends, family members, teachers, coworkers—anyone you trust—to offer some perspective on you and your actions. Ask them what you're good at. Sometimes, we can't see what's within us. This is an opportunity to get some objectivity.
- Ask yourself the following questions:
  ◦ What are some things you would do, even if you didn't get paid to do them?
  ◦ What's the most important thing on your bucket list you want to experience or accomplish?
  ◦ If you had all the money in the world, how would you spend your time?
  ◦ What would your perfect day look like?

- What habits do you have?
- What fuels you through your day?
- What are the differences between your past and now?
- Who do you want to help?
- What are some reoccurring themes in your life?
- What do you value?

MOVING FORWARD WITH COURAGE

Once you get to the heart of your why, it can be hard to find the courage to move forward with it. I invite you to see this as a time and place to start fresh rather than adhering to your old way of doing things.

When you get to this point, it can be very confronting. It's total fight or flight. You might feel encouraged to say, "Screw it. I'm going all in," then dig deep, be with the emotions that show up, and work through it. Or you might say, "Whoa, I just got way outside my comfort zone. I'm right up against something and I don't like it. It's dark. I need to go find the light switch. I'll be right back." If that's you, just remember it's OK to take a break—just don't abandon the why. Come back to it later with a fresh perspective. One thing I do is share my why with someone in my life who I know will hold me accountable and follow up with me about it.

Unfortunately, some give in to fear. They decide to never

put in the work or take the path less traveled. Those of us who have done the work know it's well worth it to fight for your passion and purpose.

PASSION AND PURPOSE

Passion and purpose go hand in hand and play a huge part in your why. If passion is the chicken, purpose is the egg. If you're passionate about something, you'll likely discover your purpose in life. People love to make "finding their passion" into something deeply complicated—it's not. **HOW TO START:** Ask yourself, "What are the things I really enjoy? What makes me come alive? What would I rather be doing than anything else in the world?" Whatever you answered to any of those questions is what you are passionate about. Your passion is already within you; you just have to discover it.

Purpose, on the other hand, is the deeper reason for your existence. It's your passion in action.

As a coach, I spend 90 percent of my time helping others figure out what truly lights them up. I have them think back in time to a moment when they felt incredible. Most can't help but smile as they explain the moment. For one of my clients, it was climbing a mountain. He described the experience and was so filled with joy. Then he asked, "But how can I make a living climbing mountains?"

When you're pinpointing your passion and purpose, you have to take money out of the equation. Worry about your passion and your purpose first, then brainstorm the creative ways you can implement them into your life.

Pay attention to your thoughts, your energy, the things that show up. If you see something or someone and you get scared or your heart races or you start to sweat or you get excited, that's your body telling you it's important. Write it down if you need to—do whatever it takes to hold on to it so you can explore it more and figure out how you can get more of it in your life.

If during this process you find there's more than one thing that makes you spark, that's perfect. Nowhere does it say you can feel excited about only one thing. In Mark Manson's book, *The Subtle Art of Not Giving a Fuck*, he says when a person asks, "What should I do with my life? What's my life purpose?" that person really is asking, "What can I do worthwhile with my time?" Manson asserts there's no reason for anyone to be constantly preoccupied with trying to figure out the cosmic significance of their lives while sitting on the couch eating Doritos; rather, we should be getting off our asses and discovering what feels important to us.

What Manson is telling us and what I'm telling you is, change takes action. You won't figure out what matters to you if you just wait around for it to come to you as you're going through life on autopilot. You have to go find it, even if you take only one small step toward it every day. If you're not doing something to change, you're doomed to keep doing the same stuff that's making you miserable in the first place (I might have said that before—and get ready, because I'm going to say it again). The smallest step in the right direction can end up being the biggest step of your life. Tiptoe if you have to, but take a step.

ADDRESSING BAD HABITS

Once you have a firm grip on why you want to do something, you have to figure out what's been keeping you from doing it up to this point. Don't get too excited—this is not pity party time (no time is pity party time). This is the time for you to look within and find those behaviors you engage in again and again that are doing nothing but holding you back.

For example, think about how you speak to others. If you're like most people, you probably offer a great deal of preamble before you speak. You might be the smartest person in the room on a subject, but you preface what you're about to say with "I might be wrong," or "This is just what I think, but..." One of my clients is the king of "I don't know." Think about what it costs you when you present yourself that way. It stems from a fear of looking stupid or bad, but it's a very safe way to live.

Most people have collected a lot of evidence to support why they're not good enough, why they don't get promoted, why they never fall in love, why they can't hold down a job, or why the world is against them. You must dismantle those stories. You can't create new stories on top of the old ones.

I've met lots of people who don't want to see anything negative in themselves. An SVP of a large tech company once came to me for some coaching, and I asked her, "Why do you believe you need a coach?"

She first responded with, "I'm not sure, but I was told I could benefit from having one." But as we dug deeper, we found she felt disconnected from others at her level.

"Well, what do you think?" I asked.

"I think I'm fine," she said. "I think people love me, and I've been told I'm bubbly. I have a great personality. I'm personable, and I light up the room."

We talked for a bit longer, and as we did, I realized she was affirming everything I said, constantly throwing out an "Uh-huh" or "Yeah, totally," even before I had finished a thought. When I finished talking, I asked, "Can you do me a favor and repeat back to me something I said?"

She did, and it wasn't even close. It was then we both

realized her "bubbly personality" was actually causing her to check out in a way. She wasn't truly listening to others; she was so busy acting engaged that she was forgetting to actually engage.

Just like this SVP, we all have the tendency to think what we perceive as our best qualities are universally appreciated. It's important to recognize we have faults, and even our talents can have drawbacks in certain scenarios. By doing so, you can catch yourself before falling into a pigeonhole. For the SVP, now she knows why she couldn't connect to others at her level. Despite having a great personality, she was never having a good enough conversation with them to understand them and connect with them. Can you think of a time when your talents actually held you back? Where were you? Who were you with? What happened? How did it impact you and those around you? Examine that—it might just be the reason you haven't reached that goal you've been chasing.

EMBRACING OBSTACLES

Another huge part of living authentically is accepting that life is rarely, if ever, going to hand you what you want. Chances are, you're going to have to fight for it, and sometimes, that can mean pushing yourself harder than you ever dreamed possible. As Thomas Edison once said,

"Many of life's failures are people who did not realize how close they were to success when they gave up."

Most great people have overcome seemingly insurmountable obstacles to get where they are today. Here are just a few of their stories that inspire me:

- Oprah Winfrey grew up in extreme poverty. She was sexually abused and got pregnant at age fourteen. Shortly after birth, her son died. When she was eventually hired by a TV station, Oprah was fired for being "unfit for television." She took that struggle, turned it into the fire that fueled her iconic career, and has become one of the most successful living women today.
- Richard Branson was a pretty bad student and battled dyslexia. He didn't get good grades and did poorly on standardized tests. Instead of giving up, he used the power of his personality to drive him to success. Today, Branson has created a powerful brand in Virgin.
- Dwayne "The Rock" Johnson is arguably one of the best wrestlers of all time and one of the biggest personalities and stars in Hollywood, but he didn't always have it so great. He faced a career-ending injury that would keep him from playing professional football. After years of paying his dues in the world of professional wrestling, he finally stepped out of the ring and onto the silver screen and became the household name we all know today.

- JAY-Z grew up in the projects. For a good portion of his life, he tried and repeatedly failed to get a record deal. After years of rejection and struggle, he took matters into his own hands. Because no one would take him on, he established his own label called Roc-A-Fella Records with his partners at the time, Damon Dash and Kareem Burke. Later, he released his first album, which went platinum, and Roc-A-Fella went on to launch the careers of some of the most popular artists of our time.
- Jim Carrey used the law of attraction to propel his success by writing himself a check for $10 million. He placed that check in his wallet and worked his ass off for seven years until he was able to cash it when he received the money for his work in *Dumb and Dumber*. But many don't know that when he was fifteen, Carrey had to drop out of school to support his family. His father was an unemployed musician, and as the family went from lower middle class to poor, they eventually had to start living in a van. Carrey didn't let this stop him from achieving his dream of becoming a comedian. When it comes to choosing not to settle for what life hands us, the acclaimed actor says, "So many of us choose our path out of fear disguised as practicality."

These people all knew that obstacles are just opportunities in disguise. We are all going to face them—and when we do, we can't be afraid of failing. I've failed plenty in my career. I have been turned down by more jobs than I can count. I've been let go. I've launched products that weren't nearly as successful as they should have been. I've been told no, not now, and no way.

In the moment, failure sucks. Rejection is terrible. We all hate it, and we're all capable of being hurt by it. It's important to recognize that and allow yourself to feel bad. Pretending you're not is inauthentic. Give yourself time to grieve or process whatever you're going through—but not too much time. Just enough to appreciate whatever you can learn from the situation, let it reshape your approach, then move on with a better perspective.

Don't bother attempting to shield yourself from future failure. If you do, it means you're not looking to grow and learn anymore. In short, you're playing it safe. When you fail, it means you're outside your comfort zone, and that is where you learn and grow.

Also, don't look to place blame anywhere but with yourself. No one wins the blame game. We inherently don't want to take accountability for our messes. People leave wakes of problems, and issues, and drama, and toxicity behind them. However, when you blame others, you're not taking responsibility for your part.

Again, looking at your drawbacks and failures is no one's

idea of fun. During my twenty years of self-improvement, I've had to turn over every stone. I've had to look at my insecurities, my arrogance, my cynicism, and all the shortcomings of being a husband, friend, father, son, brother, and coach. I've not enjoyed that. I don't readily wake up saying, "I cannot wait to find out what I'm insecure about today!" Nobody does. But at some point, you have to look at these things. If you don't, it will not only keep you living in a safe, secluded, and shallow existence, but you will also have a pile of regrets.

Instead of playing the blame game or pretending like it didn't happen, here are some questions to ask yourself the next time you fail:

- Are your expectations or goals realistic?
- Are you grateful, having failed?
- What actions are you repeating that aren't working out for you?
- Do you spend too much time complaining?
- Are your good habits outweighing your bad ones?
- Are you taking good care of your physical, mental, and emotional self?
- Are you preoccupied with thinking about the worst-case scenarios?
- Do you procrastinate?
- Do you surround yourself with more takers than givers?

- Are you making yourself a priority?
- Are you doing your best?
- Who can help you?
- What will you do next?

CHAPTER 5

POSITIVE MINDSET: ACTION, THOUGHT, AND SPEECH

I want to make the ceiling my new floor every day.

—LEWIS HOWES, *NEW YORK TIMES* BEST-SELLING
AUTHOR, TOP 100 PODCAST IN THE WORLD WITH *THE
SCHOOL OF GREATNESS*, FORMER PRO ATHLETE

As you do the work to figure out what you want and who you are, maintaining a positive mindset is critical. Bogging yourself down with negativity will get you nowhere.

Of course, life is not all unicorns and rainbows. Not everything we see and hear is going to be positive or even close to it sometimes. In the morning, you may want to wake up, yawn, say, "Namaste," and have a moment of blissful meditation, but it's much more likely you're going to rise to the sounds of sirens outside, a dog barking, an alarm going off, or your phone ringing. You can be ripped out of a positive mindset and lurched into a negative one in the blink of an eye.

HOW TO START: Anytime you notice you're about to process a negative input of some kind, make a conscious decision as to how much energy you want to put into that experience. Think about how the negativity is going to affect you. The goal is to minimize the amount of negative energy impacting you.

Outcomes are not predicated on our emotions but based on who we choose to be as human beings. Understanding who you are at your core, what you believe in, what your values are, what your passion is, and why you're doing what you're doing will all allow you to have a better handle on your life. It will help you block out some of that negativity, but because we are human, it's still bound to creep in. Let's look at a few tools that can help you kick it back out.

TEA TIME

If you ever feel yourself giving in to the negative bullshit, focus on your TEA: thoughts, emotions, and actions. If you can change one of these three things, you can influence the other two and nip some negative behaviors in the bud.

Thoughts, emotions, and actions constantly influence one another. Understanding the right relationship among them lets us choose how we want to behave and enables us to change. When we decouple our feelings from our actions, we open more possible outcomes—outcomes not predicated on our emotions but based on who we choose to be as human beings.

Our worldview is influenced by a balance between our thoughts and our emotions. When we understand what we're feeling, it helps us make better choices in life. If you think you're a failure, you're going to feel like a failure, and you're going to act like a failure, which reinforces the belief that you are indeed a failure. It's a self-fulfilling prophecy, and those are never good. The same principle also applies to being happy and great in life. If you think you're great, you're going to feel great and you're going to act great.

If you're like most people and walk around with a negative internal dialogue constantly on a loop, it's going to impact the decisions you make. When you're able to harness those thoughts and act more in line with your emotions, you become more effective in making choices in all areas of your life.

FIND THE FEELING BEHIND THE THOUGHT

Maybe you're pissed, or angry, or frustrated, and thinking, *Screw that* or *I can't believe s/he said that thing*—that's dialogue, not actual emotion. You need to stop and ask yourself why you're letting yourself think such thoughts. Doing so allows you to see things more clearly. You stop ping-ponging back and forth, and it becomes a conversation you can manage. In other words, you get a grip.

HOW TO START: For example, if you say, "I feel stupid," the feelings behind your thought could be much more than a feeling of stupidity. It could be denial, despair, or disappointment. When you can label the emotions behind the thought, you can figure out how to address them. Just thinking the thought over and over gets you nowhere.

When you are able to stop and pause and name your emotions, you can deal with them. Owning your emotions gives you something to work with; otherwise, you just remain a constant victim. Complaining is like verbal diarrhea; it just doesn't stop. Such behavior can also be intoxicating to other people who are victims, and next thing you know, you've got enablers.

We tend to accept feelings without requiring any evidence to support why we're having them. It's important to check to see if your feelings are justified and warranted. For example, if you say you feel afraid of something, check for the threat. If there's not an actual threat, find what's really going on and work on managing the feeling.

When we let our feelings go unchecked, we're giving up on ourselves. We're allowing ourselves to be seduced by those bullshit moments.

CHALLENGE YOUR BELIEFS

If you're stuck in a negative place, it helps to look for evidence to support the opposite of what you feel. If you think you're not good enough at something, go do something that helps you feel worthy—it's that simple. **HOW TO START:** It can be anything—take a walk, read something enriching, do something nice for someone else. There are an unlimited number of things you could do to put yourself in a more positive mindset.

Sometimes, you'll also have to confront yourself. When you say, "Wow, I screwed up," make it a point to respond with, "OK, now let me figure out how can I learn from this." This is way easier said than done. I've been doing this for twenty years, and I'm still in the learning phase. I am a coach who has a coach. I still throw my arms up and say, "Screw it!" I've learned I need to cycle through my disappointment, anger, frustration, cynicism, and sarcasm in order to not dwell on the things bothering me. Figure out what gets in your way, and make your unhappiness a problem you address head-on and not something you put to the side.

You have to create a more positive outlook in order to reach better outcomes. Happiness is like a muscle—the more you're committed to working on your ability to be happy, the stronger you will become.

STOP USING THESE WORDS NOW

When developing a more positive outlook, you have to eliminate self-defeating language. I call such language "bankrupt" because it completely lacks value. Let's explore a few terms and phrases I'd recommend deleting from your vocabulary:

"TRY"

As Yoda said, "Do. Or do not. There is no try." When you say, "I'll try," you aren't holding yourself accountable. You're making an excuse for why you won't do something before you even attempt to do it. "I'll try" translates to "probably not gonna happen." When you give someone your word and say you'll do something, "try" has no place in the conversation. Be firm. Commit, or don't bother.

"SHOULD"

When you say, "I should do something," you're implying you don't really want to do that thing. Or you're again implying that thing might not get done at all. "Should" is not "will." It ties a sense of shame or guilt to the action, like if you don't do it, you'll be punished in some way. Saying you should do something doesn't mean you're going to do it; it means "maybe I will, or maybe I won't, and I'll just deal with the consequences instead."

"PROBLEM"

People say, "I have a problem," and that's not necessarily a bad thing, but when somebody says they have a problem, it can feel like a lot of work to come up with a solution. That, in return, causes people to stress out, and it can block creativity.

"HARD"

A wise coach once told me that there's no such thing as "hard." You can't go to a store and buy hard. Concrete is hard. Hard is not something that can exist on its own. When you say something is going to be hard, that doesn't make any sense. Come up with a more empowering word, one with some possibility in it.

If you need a replacement word for "hard," try "challenging"—there's a word with promise. If something's a challenge, it means there's an opportunity to rise, and there's an opportunity to succeed or fail, but learn regardless.

"SOMEDAY"

Forget "someday." The last time I looked, "someday" is not in the calendar. There's Monday through Sunday, but there's not someday. Do that thing you want to do today! Or at the very least, give yourself a firm deadline and adhere to it. Because, trust me, someday ain't ever coming. Such generalizations leave room for wandering off the path to happiness. Studies have shown if you attach a time and a date to something, there's a higher probability you'll get it done.

"WISH"

"Wish" is just a subtle form of "I can't" or "I'm not worthy of." If you wish for something and wait to see how long it takes to happen, you're going to be waiting forever.

HERE'S A WORD YOU CAN USE!

Mindset expert Carol Dweck introduced the concept of the word *yet*, and how adding that simple word into your normal vocabulary can change your entire outlook. Saying

"This doesn't work yet" or "I can't do this yet" carries far more power than "This doesn't work" or "I can't do this." That one little word can take you from a closed mindset to one focused on growth.

When you have a growth mindset, you believe you're not static and that you have the aptitude and ability to change and grow.

HOW TO START: To further achieve a growth mindset, start to pay attention to what you say and how you say it. Look for patterns, and dig into the underlying beliefs hidden in those words. Are there better words you can use when you notice yourself using bankrupt language? Saying words that are more proactive and have accountability attached to them can make a huge difference in the growth of your mindset.

CHAPTER 6

HAPPINESS AND BALANCE

Be thankful for what you have; you'll end up having more. If you concentrate on what you don't have, you will never, ever have enough.

—OPRAH WINFREY, CEO, PRODUCER, PUBLISHER, ACTRESS, AND INNOVATOR

In life, we're taught to take a specific path: go to school, get a degree, get a job, buy a house, find love, and then be happy. We have the delusional mindset that we can't have happiness or even approach the concept of happiness until we've accomplished certain objectives. Says who? Such thinking is a trap, because it forces us to never live in the moment and appreciate the present. Instead, we're constantly moving on to the next thing. The hamster wheel of life starts to move, and we become content just spinning our entire lives away.

Good news: You can escape from this mindset and have happiness right this very moment. There are no predetermined standards you must reach before you can be happy. Once you adopt the mindset of "I am happy," then you can be happy. There you have it. Wasn't terribly hard, was it? The only person who needs to believe in you is you. If you believe you can be happy, then you can. Let me explain.

BE-DO-HAVE

People set up their lives to "have" something they believe they need to have before they can "do" what they feel they need to do so they can "be" happy. This is precisely the wrong order. The right order is Be-Do-Have. Your attitude (how you tend to "be") will influence your actions (what you "do"), which determine the outcomes you will achieve (or what you end up "having").

HOW TO START: To get into this proper mindset, start by asking yourself, "What's important to me, and what are the outcomes I wish to achieve?" When you look at life through this lens, you'll recognize happiness does not start with others—it starts within you.

Next, take a moment and envision happiness. What does it look like to you? Why can't you have it right now? Maybe you feel you want to be a better student, friend, family member, father, mother, husband, wife, and so on. Maybe happiness to you means achieving wealth or owning a nice car. Whatever it is, I want you to ask yourself what little changes you can make right this very moment to make your vision of happiness a reality.

Thinking about things this way might force you to break out of some routines you've been really comfortably executing for quite some time. Most of us have the unconscious desire to do what we've done for generations. We like the loop of going to school, getting a job, paying the mortgage, living the grind. Hustle becomes a badge of honor. We see happiness as a far-off thing that will take some miracle to find, when the secret to being everything you want to be is simple: just be.

If happiness for you means wealth, then do the things people with money do. Dress as well as you can, talk with confidence, carry yourself with your head held high. Educate yourself on how successful people do the things they do and start embodying them, even if you have only a dollar in your bank account. **HOW TO START:** Find a mentor, join a mastermind group or a group of like-minded people with similar goals who will support you, or find someone you want to emulate and reach out to them. Remember what Warren Buffett once said: "The best thing I did was to choose the right heroes." I also encourage you to check out Gerard Adams, The Millennial Mentor, who's all about people leveraging their passions to create lives they love.

If you can picture yourself becoming happy, you can drive yourself forward within that vision. For most people, it's going to take work to undo some of the bad habits we've had ingrained in us our entire lives.

SOMETIMES, YOU HAVE TO BAKE THE CAKE

Too many people live a life of "either/or" when we all should be living lives of "and." We think we can either have a job that allows us to retire at fifty or we can have a job we actually like. We can either devote our time to getting in shape or have time for work, family, and a social life. We've been taught again and again that we can't have our cake and eat it, too—in other words, we can't possibly get all the things we want out of life.

Guess what? You can—you just might not be able to eat the cake right away. In some cases, you're going to have to bake the cake first, but you will get to eat it eventually. When we limit our idea of happiness to only a cupcake, we are really just giving up and focusing on the cup and not the cake. Why? Because others tell us we can't do something? That's bullshit. Don't give up on your happiness just because your action scares others.

We've conditioned ourselves to believe we're not good enough, and we settle as a result. The context in which we live becomes survival and compromise rather than creation and possibility.

We start to believe certain things are impossible, which leads us to make weak choices because we don't believe we can have more than one thing at a time.

When you start to allow yourself to consider the possibility of having everything you ever wanted, your life will change. **HOW TO START:** Ask what are five things you would love to have right now in your life. List them. Now, close your eyes and visualize what that would look like. How would you feel? Where are you? This exercise will allow you to hone in on the things you are committed to and begin to accomplish more than you ever thought possible.

If you're still not convinced, ask yourself right now, "Why do I believe I can't have everything I want?" If your answer is anything close to I'm not smart enough, I'm not good enough, no one likes me, or no one's going to help me, that's all bullshit, not to mention already taken by a few million other people using the very same excuses. There's always a solution. It might not be perfect, it might not be easy, it might not appear immediately, and it might change, but there is always an answer.

I listen to people talk themselves out of doing the things they want to do, because they think with an "either/or" mindset. I've heard every excuse in the book, with money and time being the most common. It's not about money. It's not about time. It's about being committed to your dreams. Time is a fixed variable. Money comes and goes. If you're committed to it, you're going to find a way to do it, and there are ways to work with people to find a way to do it.

The process is not always going to be easy. Finding your happiness will be one of the biggest challenges you will face, but it's worth it.

THE BEST THINGS IN LIFE ARE THE THINGS YOU HAVE TO WORK FOR*

That's my nice way of saying some of this will suck.

You have to create room in your life for happiness. You can't expect your bad habits and unhealthy relationships and shitty career to work with it—you must be willing to expand and evolve. You have to be willing to address what's not working and either do something about it or ditch it altogether. Is your goal to run a marathon, but you just can't seem to kick that half-a-pack-a-day smoking habit? Are your friends bringing you down with their expectations of who you are and what you're capable of? Do you wake up every day wishing the place you work at would burn to the ground in a fiery inferno *Office Space*-style? None of that is going to fit into your new outlook of happiness and positivity, and that means you have to do something about it.

I know making such changes sounds scary and complex and challenging. I'm not going to sugarcoat it for you—it is all those things. However, it's also as simple as asking yourself the questions I've provided you throughout this book. Ask yourself what's missing from each of the four categories: finances, relationships, career, and overall wellness (**see the appendix** for some questions related to these). What do you need to do to feel fulfilled and satisfied in each of those areas?

In the end, no matter what sacrifices you have to make, you must remember it's all for your greater mental, physical, and emotional health and well-being. Years from now, you don't want to look back and say, "I wish I had done this or that." You don't want to waste any more time living a life that isn't the one you want.

Believe in yourself now. Take action now. Let's take a look at some of the ways you can do so.

A GRATEFUL MINDSET

There's a ton of power in having a grateful mindset. When you're grateful for what you have in the moment you have it, it creates a shift toward growth and a more positive mindset and you create abundance around you. Happiness begets happiness, just as misery loves company. Just ask some of the people who swear by the power of a grateful mindset: Wayne Dyer, Oprah Winfrey, Deepak Chopra, and Tony Robbins.

I've never met a miserable person who also has opportunities coming at them from every direction. Even if they've achieved some success, they remain miserable because they constantly see themselves as the victim or are just plain never satisfied. They didn't start their success on a grateful foundation—it stemmed from misery, which they allowed to percolate and fester. If you do your best to strive for happiness through gratitude, you elevate yourself and life opens up.

When it does, you have to be prepared to make the most of it. The following are my four favorite practical tips and strategies for being more productive inside of a context you create.

80/20

The rule of 80/20, or the Pareto principle, suggests 20

percent of your activities will account for 80 percent of your results. The rule is about prioritizing and focusing on the things that matter most. The activities that are most demanding also carry the highest pay-off. In other words, don't waste your energy on the smaller, more meaningless tasks when you could be using it on the big goal you've been chasing.

I've seen people become frustrated because they go about it in reverse. They work hard 80 percent of the time and see only 20 percent of results. People who are smart about how they're engaged know what they're going after and maintain their focus, knowing it's better to work smart 20 percent of their time to see as much as 80 percent in results. Check out Richard Koch's book, *The 80/20 Principle*, for more.

THE FIVE-SECOND RULE

Mel Robbins created the five-second rule, which states if there's something you really want to do, then you need to do it within five seconds of deciding you want to do it. Otherwise, your brain will decide it's not worth your time. Robbins says knowing what you will do and why you need to do it aren't enough. Instead, you need to just do it. You must launch yourself into action, because if you sit around waiting for motivation, it won't come. A year from now, you'll be in the same place you are today.

Once, I tested her rule out on a ropes course. There was a part where I had to stand on a small box fifty feet off the dirt and jump to a ring about five feet away. I climbed all the way there. Then I stood on that little square—nothing short of a gust of wind keeping me aloft—for one, two, three, four, and finally, five seconds, and I was petrified. It didn't matter that my team was cheering me on or that I was so close to victory. I ended up having to scoot on my butt and reach out in the most precarious way possible, because I let my five seconds pass. I let my brain process defeat right when I had a chance to win.

THE TWO-MINUTE RULE

The two-minute rule is designed to overcome procrastination and laziness. The rule states that if something takes less than two minutes, you should do it now. If it takes more than two minutes, you should do it later. It's pretty self-explanatory, and it works for the little things you want to accomplish, whether it's replying to an email or completing a task for a bigger goal.

THE SEINFELD STRATEGY

An interviewer once asked Jerry Seinfeld for any advice he had for young comics. He answered, "The way to be a better comic is to create better jokes, and to create better jokes, you must write every day." To hold himself to such a standard, Seinfeld had a huge calendar on his wall, which he marks with an X anytime he does his writing for that day. After a few days, he gets a chain of red Xs going, until eventually it's habit. He grows his chain, day after day, and by doing so, he gets better and better as a comedian and writer.

I love Seinfeld's technique because it's not about building a result—it's about building habits that will create a result. Finding something that's going to hook you into a repetitive motion of productivity every day can be an excellent anchor in accountability. Just remember, if everything were easy, everyone would already have everything they want. You have to be willing to put in the effort every single day.

FEAR IS YOUR FRIEND

Everyone experiences fear. Some people learn how to manage it, while others succumb to it. Regardless, most bullshit moments stem from fear—the fear of failure, of being less than something, of rejection, of being not prepared for something, of being a fraud. At the end of the day, they're all the same fear—the fear of not being good enough. It paralyzes us and keeps us from getting the things we want.

So how can you make fear work for you?

DON'T MAKE IT BIGGER THAN IT HAS TO BE

First, you must change your perception of fear. Perception is how we see and understand what's happening around us coupled with what we decide we're going to make that all mean. Our perceptions can be a source of strength or a source of weakness. Honing your perception takes discipline, and there are a few things to keep in mind when you're faced with something you fear.

HOW TO START: Focus on what can be controlled. When we feel like life is out of control, it's like the glass was half-empty, then it fell and shattered, and now the liquid is spilling all over our best pair of pants. Our brains literally go, "Holy shit!" It doesn't have to be that dramatic. Sometimes, it's just about looking for one thing you can control in that moment. Taking action will rewire your brain and calm you down. Ultimately, it's how you start to see opportunities within obstacles. You start to create hope.

DON'T FEAR FEAR

Even if it goes against everything you've been taught to believe, see fear as a good thing. If you're afraid, you're likely stepping outside of your comfort zone. It means you're attempting something new and challenging yourself in some way. Let fear be an opportunity for growth—embrace it.

I tell my clients to look for fear and move toward it. Most fear comes from worrying about the future, but you create your own future by your reaction to what's happening around you now. The only value is in focusing on the present.

I GOT NINETY-NINE PROBLEMS...BUT MOST OF THEM ARE MADE UP

Many of the things we fear never happen. Think about it: how often in your life has the worst-case scenario actually happened? Compare that with how much time you spent worrying about it. Ninety-nine percent of the things we dream up inside our heads will never, ever come to fruition, no matter how much we love to focus on irrational thoughts. Focus on the 1 percent of things that might actually happen instead.

DON'T LET YOUR FEAR DEFINE YOU

Before you can begin overcoming any kind of fear, you have to know what it is you fear most.

What exactly is it you're afraid of? Maybe look at the four areas of your life. Answering requires some vulnerability, which is why most people live a life of denial—a life of a fantasy world. They would rather spend their time creating a glossed-over version of their lives on social media than dealing with the hard truth of their realities. That's a lot easier than figuring out the root of what's holding you back.

Instead of pretending like it doesn't exist, call fear out. Name it. If you label the fear, it gives you the strength to deal with it, and when you do, you can realize you are not your fears. You experience fear, sure, but it does not define who you are. You have control over it—use it.

SHARE IT

Tell somebody what you're fearful of. As soon as you start to share what you're afraid of, it starts to take on less energy. Don't let embarrassment stop you—I promise whoever you're talking to has a ton of fears themselves. Your willingness to be vulnerable just might encourage them to do the same. It kills me as a coach to see others spend any time sweeping things under the rug. If you really want to be happy, you have to own up to your vulnerabilities. Otherwise, that pile under the rug is just going to grow and grow until you can't even walk on it anymore.

HAPPINESS IS A CHOICE

While everything we've discussed in this chapter can help you find happiness, the key to truly living a happy life, day in and day out, boils down to a choice. **HOW TO START:**

You have to ask yourself, "Am I going to be happy right now or wait?" Happiness is where you are regardless of what's happening around you, even if your world is falling apart. Your outside circumstances are going to influence you all the time in a variety of different ways. It's up to you to decide if you're going to do anything about it.

Here are a few ways you can choose to be happy:

- Stop attempting to please everybody. Wanting to be liked is in our DNA. When you're aiming just to please people, it's inauthentic. You're not being yourself, and ultimately, that's not going to generate any kind of happiness.
- Get rid of arrogance. Happy people are not arrogant people. They're just not. Happiness and arrogance are like oil and water; they can't coexist.
- Stop being a perfectionist. Perfection is a delusion. It's not possible. Stop chasing it. I don't care what Pinterest says—perfect cannot be manufactured. You will waste your life trying.
- Give up the fear of failing. If you're constantly coming from a place of "I don't want to fail," you're never going to even start pursuing your goals. Have an intention and be committed to your vision. Be flexible around what you're expecting because rarely do things end up the way we expect them to—that's not failing; that's living.

- Be in the present. Look back to your past carefully to find the lessons you need to learn, but remember, the past is a place of reference, not residence. Don't dwell there, or the present will pass you by.

CHAPTER 7

GOALS, ADVERSITY, AND SUCCESS

If you can't, you must. If you must, you can.

—TONY ROBBINS, #1 *NEW YORK TIMES* BEST-
SELLING AUTHOR, LIFE AND BUSINESS STRATEGIST,
PHILANTHROPIST, AND ENTREPRENEUR

If you're like just about every other person on the planet, you have goals. If you had to, could you explain them clearly to someone else? Sometimes, we're clear about what we want in our own minds, but we don't state our goals plainly enough to others. A rule of thumb is, if you can't explain your goal to somebody else, you likely need to rethink it.

Once you define your goals and begin to pursue them,

you're going to hit some roadblocks. You can't let adversity stand in the way—your expectations must come with an adjustment bar. There are too many people who set goals, and at the first sign of it not happening, boom, they're done.

There are also people who suffer from being too focused on their goals. They get so caught up in checking the to-dos off that they lose track of what actually matters. They become completely self-absorbed and forget to be present in life.

Finding and having success comes with these obstacles. You're going to have to set goals, but you also have to create balance. You must be able to live for your goals without your goals controlling your life. Doing so requires navigating around some potential pitfalls as you pursue the things you want. Goals typically go unfulfilled because of two things: unclear expectations and thwarted intentions.

WHAT TO EXPECT WHEN YOU EXPECT SOMETHING

Unclear communication starts wars. Just look at the state of the world right now—we live in a very divisive country and a huge contributing factor to that is a lack of clear communication around people's expectations.

An expectation is a strong belief something's going to

happen. An expectation has a success or a failure attached to it, depending on whether that expectation is realized. When we have an expectation, whether it's communicated or not, the universe doesn't just say, "Hey, you've got an expectation. That's awesome. Let me fulfill it." That's not how it works. It's not like there are three wishes and a genie sitting on your desk. If everybody's expectations were fulfilled, we'd all be skinny, smart, healthy, and rich. That's just not the way it works. You will bump up against reality.

Just as you need to clearly define your goals, you also must clarify your expectations. They fail to serve us when they are not communicated. You have to be able to speak them to others. Otherwise, you risk mistaking your expectations for reality and all but guarantee disappointment and an intense feeling of disempowerment when things don't go the way you expected them to.

WHAT ARE YOUR INTENTIONS?

Intention is something we want or plan to do. When you set your intention toward a goal while being detached from the end result, you can pay full attention to what you're doing. Being intentional means being open to the possibility of a different outcome. There's an opportunity to learn, to grow, to go outside your comfort zone, and develop some new skills.

Setting the intention and then letting go of the attachment to a specific desired outcome allows you to cultivate mindfulness about your day-to-day efforts.

Think about sports. Athletes play a series of games over and over. Each individual game, depending on the sport, may not mean much in the moment, but it will later when it comes to rankings. An athlete's focus is on the game at hand, but the desired outcome is to win a championship. If they're constantly thinking about the championship, the likelihood that they're going to be focused on what's in front of them is small.

Intention is an impulse. It gives structure and direction to the energetic forces, the curiosity and the creativity. **Here are a few pointers on becoming more intentional:**

- Have clarity about your values, what you believe in, and what makes you be your best. In other words, be clear on who you are. If you don't like vegetables, don't go to the farmer's market. If you hate jogging, find a new exercise regime. Be intentional with your time. It's that simple.
- Think about the expectations you have about yourself and about others. How do you think your life is supposed to be or supposed to work? Ask yourself, are those expectations serving you? If not, get new ones or better define the ones you have so they are more in line with the vision of life you see for yourself.

- Realize that your life is made up of choices. Every morning is a new day full of decisions and opportunities. You get to choose your mindset and your decisions. You don't have to let the circumstances of your past derail your present or your future. You have a choice in the matter. Realize that every morning is a new opportunity.

GOAL SETTING

Once you understand your expectations and intentions, you can set realistic goals. **HOW TO START:** Think SMART—Is it a Specific goal? Is there some way to Measure it? Is it Achievable? Is it Relevant? Is it Time-based?

You have to know how you plan to set out to achieve your goal, how long you're willing to work for it, and how much you are willing to sacrifice to get it. If you can't get answers to these questions, you're not ready. **See the worksheet in the appendix** to help you start.

Finally, you will need a strong support structure around you that can handle the weight of the goal. Without one, you might as well be building a skyscraper out of Dixie cups—the foundation is useless and nothing's going to hold. You have to be able to look to others for help and support when necessary. **HOW TO START:** Go back to your list of people and share with them your dreams, vision, or goals. If their reaction is anything other than excitement or support, you may want to rethink your list. Otherwise, you put yourself inside a bubble filled with nonrealistic expectations.

DO IT ALREADY

You've thought about your expectations and intentions. You've asked yourself all the relevant questions, and you have a strong support structure in place. Now it's time to go after what you want. People throw words like *hustle* and *grind* around all the time, but at the end of the day, the only thing that matters when it comes to achieving goals is smart and consistent action.

Here are some ways you can plan your work and work your plan:

- Make a schedule and stick to it. Having a clear plan for each day helps you be intentional and focus when you're at your best. I like to schedule my day the night prior so I wake up knowing exactly what I need to do that day to help get me closer to my goals.
- Write down the top five things you need to knock out and put most of your energy into those things. Do not let unimportant tasks sideline you.
- Make time blocks and decide when you will work and when you won't. Breaks are important. Anyone can

relate to how frustrating getting stuck on a singular task for an extended period can be. I like to spend about fifteen minutes fully focused. Then I take two minutes for a break. Small breaks make it easier for your brain to continue onward. Figure out what rhythm works best for you, and set yourself a timer if you need to.

· Limit your distractions. Yes, this means no Facebook, no Twitter, no Instagram, no online shopping. You might even consider silencing your phone or (gasp of absolute horror!) turning it off altogether. You will survive not knowing what your seventh-grade lab partner had for lunch, I promise.

· For more ideas around time management, check out my website.

LEAP BEFORE YOU LOOK

No, that's not a misprint, and no, I'm not saying you should just barrel into any situation completely unprepared and with no thinking. Sometimes you should, but those situations are few and far between. In most cases, I believe you should consider LEAP first: Leverage, Envision, Action, and Purpose.

LEVERAGE YOUR RESOURCES

Think about who and what you have in your life that will help you reach your goals. Think of the tactical and practical and make a list. Who are the people you will fall back on for support and motivation? Who do you know who might make a good connection? Look to create accountability through partnerships. Nothing moves without taking action, but you need the support from your resources, too.

You can also look to what's available to you in the form of resources such as podcasts or subscriptions. There is a wealth of information available at all our fingertips; dig in and see what's most helpful to you. **Some of my favorite resources are included in the back of the book.**

ENVISION YOUR GOAL

Train your brain to see what it is you want to achieve before you even begin to act on it. Picturing yourself achieving something great will propel you forward. I'm reminded of my trainer who encouraged me to see myself crossing the finish line before I trained for my first marathon. When you start out with such a positive outlook, the goal becomes clearer and more tangible in your mind. **HOW TO START:** Close your eyes and visualize yourself achieving your goal. Where are you? Who are you with? What are you wearing? Got it?

TAKE ACTION, BUT ALSO TAKE BREAKS

Create a time line, commit to it, and reward yourself. A

lot of people don't reward themselves, because they feel like they didn't earn it or deserve it, or that they failed. I'm not saying go out and buy yourself a fancy car, but maybe go see a movie, read a book, get a massage—take some time off. Let your brain recuperate, but make sure you get back to it.

HAVE PURPOSE

We discussed passion and purpose in chapter four, but just to refresh—without passion, the drive, you may never find your purpose. In this case, I want you to match your passion to your intention. Life is life. There are going to be distractions, but when you set your life up in a way that mitigates those potential distractions, it leaves you with space to show up and create your goals.

It's all about experimentation. You must be unafraid to fail. If you do fail, think about failure as falling forward. Remember, most people who have gone on to do great things with their lives are also experts in failure. The rate at which you fail is equivalent to the rate at which you grow and learn.

THE CHOICE IS YOURS

Everything I'm asking you to do in the chapter comes down to choices. After all, life is just a series of choices strung together that got you to this point. You are choosing all the time—so often, in fact, that you're probably not aware of all the choices you make.

Decision making can be tricky business. Most of the time, it can be confusing, emotional, even irrational. Economist Herbert Simon coined the term *satisficing* to describe an approach to decision making that prioritizes an adequate solution over an optimal solution. Author and blogger Gretchen Rubin talked about these kinds of decision makers in a post she called "The Happiness Project."

Rubin said, "Satisficers are those who make a decision or take action once their criteria are met." That doesn't mean they'll settle for mediocrity; the criteria could be high. But as soon as they find whatever it is they're looking for, they're satisfied, period. Simon also says there are "maximizers" who want to make optimal decisions. Even if they find what they're looking for, they are going to keep doing research, and they can't or won't decide until they've examined every option.

Basically, when you're gathering conditional information, it always comes at a cost. **But good news again: there are some practical ways to make better choices.**

- Get perspective. When it comes to making any big life change, or even some small decisions, it can get overwhelming. So get some distance. Pull away from the emotional side, so you can make more of a rational decision and analyze these things with more objectivity.

· Consider all your options. What are the alternatives? Don't allow yourself to feel trapped.
· Make a pros and cons list.
· Be aware of what you want.
· Ask for advice, but make your own choice.
· Give yourself deadlines.
· Listen to your gut.
· Don't fear the consequences.
· Stay in the present.
· Consider changing your environment.
· Take time—at least a moment—before making a decision.

HEAD VERSUS HEART

Some people are ruled by their hearts; others are ruled by their heads. The key, when it comes to making really smart decisions, is to understand what type of person you are and figure out how to balance the two. Most decisions require a little bit of both. Your head and your heart are attached, but sometimes the wiring gets crossed. If you're ruled by your gut and tend to be an impulsive person, give yourself some time to let your head catch up before you make a decision. If you're typically calm and more cerebral, tap into more emotion.

If you've allowed either your head or your heart to lead you in the wrong direction in the past, give yourself a break. As much as we don't want to dwell on the shitty stuff we've done, learning from it is how we grow. When you don't learn from your past, you're doomed to repeat it. It's why people have victim complexes, and the same bad relationships, the same crappy jobs, and the same terrible bosses again and again and again. People move to different countries to change their lives and nothing is any different because while their environment is new, they are the same. You cannot escape your own shadow—it's impossible. The quicker you're able to learn from your past mistakes, the better.

Once you learn from your mistakes, you can let them go—not any sooner. You're not defined by your past unless you say you are. If you want to carry every mistake with you for the rest of your life, you're just going to bring the same mistakes into your future. Leave the past in the past where it belongs.

HOW TO START: Instead, focus your awareness on the present. When you increase your level of awareness, you decrease the possibility for poor decisions because you have more clarity around what's going on. You can be more objective.

We are intuitive beings. When making choices, trust your

own intuition. Harness that mindfulness, awareness, and presence. Much of life is about trusting your gut. Trust that there's an answer and that you will find it. You may not know how you're going to get there, but start by trusting the process. The simple act of believing will help you move into action.

Nothing is going to happen—no matter how many times you read this book or any others—if you don't take action.

CHAPTER 8

RELATIONSHIPS: WITH SELF AND OTHERS

Be impeccable with your word. Don't take anything personally. Don't make assumptions. Always do your best.

—DON MIGUEL RUIZ, AUTHOR OF *THE FOUR AGREEMENTS*

You're probably sick of me talking about how your relationships play a big part in your overall happiness by now, but it's a point worth drilling into your brain. You have to understand that how you interact with others can tell you a lot about yourself—and how you treat yourself can tell you even more.

All most of us want in life is to have healthy, fulfilling relationships where we feel loved, safe, and/or appreciated. Such relationships—the win-win kind where all parties get something from the deal—require cooperation, communication, and understanding.

MAKE ROOM FOR RELATIONSHIPS

To have strong relationships, both personally and professionally, you have to know what the other person needs. You must listen and give the gift of presence, something that costs nothing but can be worth more than any dollar amount. Presents are great in relationships, but presence is better. In other words, make the actual relationship your priority.

In my twenty years of working with people, I've fielded the same complaint more times than I can count. They say, "I'm having issues in my relationship," or more importantly, "I want to be in a relationship, but I'm struggling to do so." I'll listen to these people explain their days to me, how almost all twenty-four hours is completely dedicated to them, them, them—and I want to shout, "That's why!" They set zero time aside for any person to have a remote chance of showing up and having a shot in their life.

So ask yourself:

- Are you one of these types of people?
- Are you caught up in your own world?
- Are you willing to make room for others?

If finding and nurturing relationships are important to you, find a way to create space in your life for having them. **HOW TO START:** Think of it this way: Why do you get out of bed in the morning? Is it because of work? Yes, because if you don't, what happens? You get fired. So keeping your job is a priority, and getting out of bed is a requirement of tending to that priority. You already know how to keep priorities—you can apply the same approach to securing and maintaining relationships.

All of this is going to take patience—something few, if any, of us are good at. When you're dealing with people, you're dealing with many variables, but if you're in the relationship for the long run, then you're going to have to be patient and sort through it all. Relationships of substance and value take time.

LISTEN UP

Relationships also require clear communication. We humans don't listen well. Did you get that? Instead, we listen to respond. We're not listening for the sake of listening; we're not listening for the opportunity; we're not listening for possibility. All we want to do is ping-pong back and forth with a bunch of uh-huhs and yeahs.

Such nonlistening is incredibly disrespectful to the other person. By not really hearing what the person is saying, you have no real understanding of what they want and need. Their expectations of you are unclear.

To clarify expectations, especially in a romantic relationship, you must be able to walk away from a conversation knowing exactly what was said (and not said) and what the other person wants. Sound like work? It's only work if your relationship is a job. Trust me, clarifying expectations will save you a lot of time.

YOU CAN'T CHANGE OTHERS (SERIOUSLY, DON'T EVEN BOTHER)

It also helps to acknowledge, respect, and honor differences. You have to be able to respect people both for who they are and for who they're not. We tend to impose on others our own ideas of how we want them to be or how we think they should be. It's extremely unfair. Not only have we not verbalized what our expectations are, but we also expect them to magically fulfill them without even knowing what they are. It's a recipe for doomed relationships.

Ask yourself, "Am I holding this person in a regard that maybe they're not capable of?" If the person isn't capable of everything you expected, that doesn't mean you should attempt to change them. It just means they're never going to become the version of themselves you have in your mind; you have to be willing to accept that or move on.

The truth is, you can't change or "fix" anybody. If you want to fix something, go find an appliance. If you want to change something, change your outfit. Doing either to a person is not fair and just going to end in disaster. People are who they are. If you're in a relationship with somebody, it has to be about honoring and respecting who they are and who they're not. You can elevate a person by helping them be best version of themselves that they possibly can be, but that's not the same as changing them—that's just accentuating what's great already about them.

This doesn't mean people can't change or shouldn't change, but it's rarely up to you to tell them to do it. If you're truly interested in helping someone who's asked for help changing, that's different. Then there's a dialogue and an opportunity to engage. But don't assume someone needs—or wants—to change.

The only person you can change is yourself. Go see how that works instead.

LESS BULLSHIT = BETTER RELATIONSHIPS

Are there any relationships in your life that no longer serve you? If you really think about it, there probably is. There's probably a few. Every once in a while, you might think, *Why do I bother keeping this person around?* Relationships are truly about give and take, and when you have a relationship in your life where you're giving and not receiving, that's bullshit.

A relationship should be a healthy exchange between two people. It's not always going to be fifty-fifty—the scale of who needs a little more from the other person is going to tip to one side occasionally, but it should always eventually return to center.

I've been there. I've had to take a hard look at some of the people in my life and decide if I really needed them or not. The list of people I've considered friends—both personal and professional—has changed greatly over the years. Some people who were in my life for many years were the ones I thought had my back and were my truest of true friends; they were also some of the first people to leave me when times got tough.

The key is, when you're thinking about a relationship with yourself and other people, don't skip out on what your gut and instinct are telling you. If you think there's a relationship in your life that's not authentic, examine if you really need it. Why put your energy into something that's basically worthless when you could be investing more time in other relationships that help you be the best, most authentic version of yourself possible?

RELATIONSHIP KILLERS

If you are nurturing a healthy relationship, beware: there are multiple ways it can be derailed, and some of them creep in without your even noticing. The following are some big ones you should steer clear of.

DEFINING SOMEONE BY THEIR PAST

We all have a past and we all attempt to cover it up, but few of us succeed. There are many ways the past can show up in your present. But here's the thing: the past is not who you are. It's a part of who you were, but it shouldn't define who you are. When you only relate to people through their pasts, you aren't giving them an opportunity to show up in the present. It's that simple. Don't judge somebody before they even have a chance to show you who they are today. Recognize them just as you recognize your own past—as a part of you but not all of you.

SELFISHNESS AND EGO

Neither of these two has a place in a good relationship. If you're being self-serving, and you're constantly worried about how you're showing up in the relationship, then you're not giving enough focus to the other person. Selfishness and ego aren't healthy, but they are part of who we are, so they're not going anywhere. You have to be actively and mindfully aware of them, otherwise they will damage your relationship. Think of it this way: if you're putting yourself first, you're putting the other person second. Is that how you'd want to be treated? Of course, you have to take care of yourself, but there is a fine line between being self-absorbed and self-care.

STRESS

Stress is the number one killer of relationships. The number one cause of stress is a lack of communication. We all have stress, and unfortunately, very few of us are any good with dealing with it. So how do you eliminate the stress? Talk to the person. Communication is the key tenet of a healthy relationship. If you're not talking to the other person, then who are you talking to? Yourself. And if you're attempting to work through a problem that involves two people, talking to yourself doesn't help.

TECHNOLOGY

Technology can be a big enemy of the modern-day relationship. Next time you go out, take a look around. I bet you'll notice at least one couple sitting together while both are on their phones. They're sitting across from each other, although they might as well be ten booths away, because they are both far too busy messing around on their phones to even notice another human presence. Unless you're managing some massive crisis, get off your phones! Create some boundaries with technology. Whether you decide there will be certain hours of the day with no electronics at home or if you put your phones in a basket at the dinner table, or whatever, just do something so a device is not preventing you from actually communicating.

OPEN YOUR HEART

Healthy relationships also require a healthy dose of vulnerability. Vulnerability is often seen as a flaw, but as Brené Brown says, "Vulnerability sounds like truth and feels like courage. Truth and courage aren't always comfortable, but they are never weakness." Your most joyful moments show up when you're being vulnerable.

Think about the times when you've been the happiest, whether it was the birth of your child or a milestone birthday party, or celebration of something you accomplished. In all of these scenarios, you were just present, completely in the moment.

Vulnerability leads to intimacy, which people avoid like the plague. Intimacy is so powerful that most people can't be with it. Think about the last time you were truly intimate with somebody—and I'm not talking about physical intimacy. I mean emotionally intimate. Can you even remember the last time? Most people would either say, "I don't know what you're talking about" or "I don't remember." That's because a lot of people don't have intimacy in their lives at all.

Vulnerability is more of a heart-to-heart principle than a head-to-head principle. Everyone is great at having head-to-head conversations. We all know how to go back and forth and talk and circle the drain for hours about a topic without ever really getting to the core of it.

When you ask someone, "How does that actually make you feel?" you're asking them to explore the emotional component at play. This is where vulnerability and intimacy exist, and you're not going to find either in your head. They're in your heart.

True heart-to-heart conversations are as about as authentic as you can get. It's not a debate or a matter of spewing out a bunch of facts to impress the other person. You're not aiming to win. Remember, if you're winning, someone else is losing.

SET SOME BOUNDARIES

Setting healthy emotional boundaries is critical to the survival of any relationship. Think of your boundaries like a property line: where would you place your "no trespassing" signs? Personal boundaries can be challenging to define, because there are no definitive lines. Even if there were, those lines are changing all the time. They're different to every person in every relationship.

Regardless of how tricky it might be, it's important to define where you end and where others begin. Such boundaries will help you decide, first and foremost, what type of people you want in your life. They'll make you ask yourself, "What kind of partner do I want? What kind of behavior am I willing to accept? What don't I want people to do to me? What do I have the right to ask for?"

Without these boundaries, you risk allowing your partner's emotional state to dictate your level of happiness or sadness. You will start sacrificing your goals and aspirations to please others. By setting boundaries, you protect your self-esteem and allow your physical, emotional, and mental state to flourish within the relationship. In other words, you'll be a lot happier.

Also, when you're clear on your boundaries, you can avoid a lot of miscommunication and confrontation. Boundaries help set expectations from the onset.

THE BEST PITY PARTY EVER

In order to be present and engaged in healthy relationships, we can't let the times we feel sorry for ourselves consume too much of our time especially in the presence of the other person. We all have an inner victim, but our egos rarely let it see the light of day. There can be value in embracing your inner victim. If you're going to be a victim, you might as well own it. Throw the pity party, take the time to feel sorry for yourself, and talk to people who will commiserate with you (remember those enablers we mentioned earlier?). Do all of this knowing that the pity party must and will end. Don't turn your own self-pity into an ongoing conversation. If you do, it will degrade every happy moment in your life.

If you feel like you're at the pity party and for some reason you can't find your coat and keys to leave, you have to figure out a way out of there. First, figure out what hold it has on you, then release yourself from it. No matter how good the attention may feel, you must move on. Take responsibility. Blaming others or outside forces will not make a difference. Whatever happened that's making you play victim is over. It happened, and it's never going to change. Let it go.

Instead, find more room for gratitude in your life. Don't let that one bad moment define every other aspect of your life. Sometimes, doing so will require forgiveness, either of someone else or of yourself. Allow yourself to be vulnerable, suck it up, and move on. No one likes the guy who stays at the party too long.

GENERATING SELF-CONFIDENCE

Everyone would like to be more confident. Let's face it, we're all insecure about at least one (and I am being generous here) thing about ourselves and our lives. I think many people see being confident as either a faraway land they'll never reach or a place where arrogance lives. Herein lies the challenge: neither of those options is too appealing, so as a result, people look at having a lack of confidence as a life sentence or, in some cases, a death sentence. Generating confidence has been written about for as long as I've been able to read and there are numerous studies out there, but here's what you need to know.

Your confidence will develop just like a muscle in your body. It grows (and shrinks) in direct response to the level of performance required of it. Either you use it or you lose it.

The good news is, you don't have to look for confidence because you already have it. You don't have to be arrogant when you embody it. Instead, opt to be grateful that you were able to accomplish something that led to your newfound confidence. Again, building your confidence will only come from taking action, and yes, this means once again stepping outside your comfort zone.

Here are some easy and practical tips for boosting your self-confidence:

- Put yourself together, e.g., dress well.
- Get to know yourself better.
- Look for little wins throughout the day.
- Emulate people you admire; research how they do what they do.
- Be kind.
- Do something for a stranger expecting nothing in return.
- Be prepared, e.g., at work.
- Learning something new every day.
- Get out of your own head and be of service to someone else.
- Do some exercise. The physiological effects will leave you feeling great.
- Attend a networking event and focus on how you can support other people rather than focusing on yourself.
- Look at a great win or success you've experienced and give yourself credit for your part in it.
- Do one thing each day that makes you smile (on the inside or on the outside).
- Switch off your autopilot and make deliberate decisions based on what really matters to you.
- Being confident sometimes looks like admitting you were wrong; be open to that possibility and embrace it should it arise.
- Trust your intuition.
- Don't feel like you have to do everything by yourself. Sometimes, the most confident thing to do is ask for help.

- Take a chance on something tomorrow—anything, big or small. Just take a chance.
- Finally, remember the words of the monk Thich Nhat Hanh: "To be beautiful means to be yourself. You don't need to be accepted by others. You need to accept yourself."

CHAPTER 9

FINDING INSPIRATION AND CHOOSING WISELY

To be yourself in a world that is constantly trying to make you something else is the greatest accomplishment.

—RALPH WALDO EMERSON

Despite growing up with artists in my family, no one ever pushed me in front of an easel or shoved a sketchbook in my hands. I was drawn to those things on my own. I felt naturally hardwired for it and enjoyed it. Along the way, my curiosity and desire to understand how things work helped me find inspiration. My whole life, I enjoyed building things and taking them apart. I had started out doing it with artwork, fascinated with the way certain colors or shapes worked together to create something interesting or beautiful. Then I started applying the same form of analysis to people. Much of that is why I am where I am today.

Life is all about the outside influences we take in. There is one trait all of the most successful people on the planet share: a quest for learning and for wanting more. They actively seek inspiration. When you're curious, you become engaged, and you become inspired, and in turn, you become more productive. Inspired people are intrinsically more motivated; they are not lazy.

We tend to spend so much time attempting to please others at the cost of feeling free and living authentically. The fear of being judged keeps us from being inspired, because we stop getting curious. We stop asking questions. Such behavior always brings us back to the safer options, usually the things we've already been doing, which is confining, not to mention incredibly boring. Inspiration doesn't grow there.

It's important to keep pushing yourself outside of your comfort zone. Find inspiration. It lies everywhere—you don't have to go far.

FEAR AND INSPIRATION DON'T MIX

When I was a young artist, I got frustrated. I used to spend hours in my room drawing, or painting, or building something; then I'd break it apart or rip it up and throw it away. My parents were always saying, "We'd love to see what you've worked on." I'd answer, "It sucked. It's not here." I was so embarrassed. I didn't want anybody to see anything I made.

After a while, I realized I had to push through the embarrassment. My fear of not being good enough suppressed my innovation and ultimately my confidence and happiness. At a young age, that's debilitating. It can grow with you and stifle you for the rest of your life.

My fear taught me to be patient. Now I set aside time to do something new and creative every day. Every week, I look to embrace a new, healthier habit or mindset that will help me improve my life.

You can do the same thing by making time to simply be creative or engage in anything that inspires you. You could make something, watch something, or learn something. Think about a time in the past you had success, or you were happy, and re-create that. Maybe even make a list and jot these memories down. The key is to keep doing it consistently, and you will soon find yourself eager to do new things and continue growing. **There are many ways and places to start. Here are just a few:**

- Watch a TED video to learn about inspiring ideas.
- Disconnect from tech and write in a journal.
- Search for social media posts with the hashtag #inspiration.
- Go for a walk in nature.
- Meditate or practice yoga.
- Discover one new skill or strength you have each day.
- Take pictures of everything that looks beautiful to you.
- Practice deep breathing.
- Notice what matters to someone else and focus solely on how they experience it.
- Listen to music that moves you.
- Read blogs written by people who have overcome adversity in their lives.
- Browse through inspirational quotes online.
- Teach someone to do something (this also works great for building self-confidence).

You can also find inspiration in people. Ask the people around you what they're grateful for. Gratitude can be incredibly inspiring. Ask people to tell you about the things they love or about something they've recently learned. You can ask somebody who knows you to tell you about your past. Spending time with your loved ones can generate a special kind of inspiration.

Finally, don't rush it and make it a to-do. Trying too hard to find inspiration or come up with some big idea will end up with your being stressed over a half-ass idea at most. Don't overthink it. Just take action and be with what develops. Who knows? You may just surprise yourself.

ACTING "AS IF"

Earlier, I shared with you a quote from another coach who changed my life: "There is no dress rehearsal." In other words, you should treat every day as if it's your last day alive. You have to ask yourself, "How can I live today without regrets?" Then live your life in terms of what you want to be remembered for. Think about the big picture. **HOW TO START:** What do you stand for? Life is short. Are you willing to spend it settling for shitty jobs and shittier relationships? You don't have to, but as I've told you again and again, you have to be the one to pull yourself out of that rut.

Acting "as if" is about living a faith-based life, not an evidence-based life, and that has nothing to do with church. It's about being what you believe. If you want to be successful, dress like successful people do. If you want to run a *Fortune* 500 company, look at the habits of the presidents and CEOs of the business giants and emulate them. If you want to be an expert in something, study it until you know it backward and forward. Make the time, make the commitment, and just do it.

Acting "as if" is also about finding the root cause of your

desire. It's not about the thing you want; it's about the emotion driving you to pursue it. Once you've identified that emotion, you can start becoming aware of how it shows up in all the areas of your life. Then, to quote a phrase you might have heard once or twice in your life, "Just do it." Just go live to the best of your ability and act "as if" the things you want are already a reality (remember the Be-Do-Have?). This is not about playing make-believe; it's about figuring out what it's going to take to get you the thing you want and doing those things no matter what.

YOU GET TO DECIDE

How you live each and every day of your life is 100 percent entirely up to you. My father used to ask me, "What kind of day are you going to have?" And I still think about that all the time—it's up to us to own the day or let it own us.

Living each day the way you want to will not happen without challenge. There is an endless list of bullshit you can decide to focus on. Finding something to complain about is the easiest thing in the world, and we love doing it. We're hardwired to complain relentlessly. But you don't have to. When that thought comes up, you can choose to focus on something more positive. Again, the choice is yours. Life is made up of a series of choices, and whether you know it or not, every single one you make contributes to who you are and the happiness that shows up within you and your life. Be aware, and don't let opportunities to create a better life for yourself pass you by. They're happening all the time.

CHANGE YOUR RELATIONSHIP WITH TIME

As you approach the end of this book, I hope you're excited to start applying all the new things you've learned. I also know there still might be a little voice in your head saying, "How in the world am I going to find the time to do all this?" Everyone gets the same twenty-four hours in a day—it's what you do with them that makes you more or less productive. Saying "I don't have the time" really means, "I'm not committed to it." If you're really in this, you have to change your relationship with time.

Do a time audit with pen and paper to find out what's robbing you of your time. Write down everything, from errands to thoughts that run through your mind. You can't manage your time if you don't know where it's spent. I call the things that suck time away from you and pull focus from the things you really want to be doing "time bandits." Once you understand how much these time suckers are costing you, you can decide how to handle them. Many of them can probably be eliminated altogether. If it's not contributing to the vision of the life you want for yourself, it's not worthy of your time. Period.

Follow these tips to get started:

- Know your goals—for the day, week, month, or even year. If you don't know where you are headed, you will most likely stop prematurely.
- Stephen Covey, coauthor of the book *First Things First*, popularized an organizational tool for your to-do list based on how important and urgent tasks are. He suggests looking at what goes into making up your day and asking where your activities fit into these categories:
  - Important and urgent—Tasks that must be done. Do them right away.
  - Important but not urgent—Tasks that appear important but on closer examination aren't. Decide when to do them.
  - Urgent but not important—Tasks that make the most "noise" but, when accomplished, have little or no lasting value. Delegate these if possible.
  - Not urgent and not important—Low-priority stuff that offer the illusion of being busy. Do them later.
  - Now write down your three or four "important and urgent" tasks that must be addressed today. As you complete each one, check it off your list. This will provide you with a sense of accomplishment and can motivate you to tackle less essential items.
- Extra credit: Always plan out your day the night before. This will, in turn, prevent you from spinning

your wheels in the morning and allow you to create a more powerful and empowering morning routine.

- Set time limits for your tasks. This will keep you intentional while ensuring you don't eat into your next task.
- Learn to say no. This can't be overstated enough. Don't take on more than you can handle. Saying no for the sake of saying yes to yourself and the task at hand is well worth it. You can always say, "Not now" instead of "No," but the key is to focus on what's in front of you, not ahead or behind you.
- Having a clock nearby in your line of sight is important to remember where you are in your day and to make sure you don't get lost.
- Focus and limit your distractions. This is a no-brainer for many, but for some, it's worth repeating. Take anyone or anything that's going to keep you from focusing on the task in front of you and eliminate it. One of the easiest ways to do this is close the browser tabs to other windows open in the background, especially if it's social media.
- Because you can't do everything, learn to prioritize the important and let go of the rest. Apply the 80/20 principle we discussed earlier.
- Delegate. If there are things that can be better done by others or things that are not so important, consider delegating. This takes a load off, and you can focus on the important tasks.
- Simplify your life by prioritizing what's most import-

ant to you and devoting the bulk of your time to it. By being relentless in your pursuit of what's important to you, you will avoid settling and create real fulfillment. Remember, you can have your cake and eat it, too. You just have to believe you are worth it, set up a support structure, communicate your wants and expectations clearly, and realize there will be sacrifices and tradeoffs along the way.

- Help yourself stay on track by writing down the top three things you want to get done today. Then eliminate all distractions and do them. Don't allow for any excuses. It really is that simple.

THE WORST REGRET OF ALL

If you've already figured out that you're not living an authentic life, good news: you don't have to waste one more minute on it. Because the worst thing that can happen is, you look back on the whole of your time on Earth and realize you did not spend any of it living authentically.

I encourage you to get the most out of your life now, because there may not be a tomorrow. There's no point in waiting for the perfect outfit, or the perfect selfie, or the perfect anything—none of it exists. Act now so you can move forward knowing you didn't waste any more time than you had to.

HOW TO START: Think about what's important to you.

Think about your values. How do you want your life to touch other people? What would make you proud? If you could do just one thing to improve the planet right now, what would it be?

At the end of the day, what is the mark you want to leave? Figure out the answers to these questions, make a plan to bring your vision to fruition, and act on it today.

You don't have one more minute to waste on any of the bullshit.

CONCLUSION

You are 100 percent responsible for your life. You can be anything you want to be. You can start over anytime.

I repeat:

You are 100 percent responsible for your life. You can be anything you want to be. You can start over anytime.

Why not now?

This book and all others out there will do nothing for you if you don't act on what you found in the pages. Change is not about the information you take in—it's about what you do with the information. You can watch every TED Talk, read every blog post, scan every list, but if you don't apply the thing you learned, it will never matter.

What you do with this book is up to you. If there was something here that really called out to you or lit a fire somewhere inside you, start there. If you still feel lost, start with discovering your passion and your purpose. The key is living your life, the one you want to live, and not settling for anything less. There is a passion and a purpose we all innately possess, and it starts with asking the right questions of self-discovery and self-transformation.

As a coach, I believe we all have the answers inside of us. We just don't know where to look. Hopefully, this book has given you clarity on where to start. **If you want to learn more, you can find me at:**

- www.joshhmiller.com
- On Twitter @coachjhm
- Facebook.com/coachjoshmiller
- www.linkedin.com/in/joshuahmiller

This is my commitment—what's yours?

I want you to have the life you want. Let's work together to help you get it. If you're ready to cut out the crap, reach out to me. I'm committed to helping everyone, including you, live a bullshit-free life. If there's an area of your life you want to work on, reach out to me for a complimentary, twenty-minute consultation. Seriously. Go to my website, click on the Book tab, check out the terms and conditions, and if it interests you, let's get started.

I'm ready when you are.

Be who you are and say what you feel, because those who mind don't matter and those who matter don't mind.

—DR. SEUSS

ACKNOWLEDGMENTS

If you told me ahead of time how challenging it would be to write this book, I probably would have passed. I'm so thankful I didn't, but I'm more thankful for the incredibly passionate, brilliant, and supporting cast of characters I had in my corner throughout the process.

Tom, your ability to synthesize what felt like one long run-on thought into a coherent and articulate outline is nothing short of a miracle. Thank you for listening.

If this was a boxing match, Coleen, you were my cut man and sparring partner. Each step of the way, you were there shadowing me and making sure I didn't take any shortcuts and kept my chin up. Thank you for being a constant voice of reason and for not throwing in the towel on me.

Thank you, Shaun, for taking a risk on me and my vision. Without your support, this book wouldn't have gotten off the ground.

Rachel, your brilliance and ability to understand my voice is pure magic. Thank you for playing this game with me.

Uncle Marshall, you may have left us in physical presence, but your smile and spirit remains in us all, while your reach is infinite. Thank you for being there for me and my family when family was the only thing that mattered. I miss you dearly and am eternally grateful for having you in my life.

To everyone else I didn't mention specifically—my friends, extended family members, clients, colleagues, coaches, authors, teachers, strangers, teams, and anyone else I missed—you have either directly or indirectly supported me in writing this book. Along my life's journey and experiences, you were there as part of the cast, and I am better for it. Thank you.

Last, to my parents who raised me in a home with love, possibility, and encouragement no matter what, thank you for doing everything imaginable to give me and Jason the opportunities to be the men we are today. Eternally grateful.

APPENDIX

ADDITIONAL RESOURCES

ON THE WEB:

- https://brendon.com
- https://tim.blog
- https://www.mindbodygreen.com
- https://tinybuddha.com
- https://jamesclear.com
- https://michaelhyatt.com
- https://addicted2success.com
- https://www.bakadesuyo.com
- https://blog.bulletproof.com
- https://www.scienceofpeople.com

BOOKS:

- *The Four Agreements: A Practical Guide to Personal Freedom*, by Don Miguel Ruiz
- *Ask and It Is Given: Learning to Manifest Your Desires*, by Esther and Jerry Hicks
- *10% Happier: How I Tamed the Voice in My Head, Reduced Stress without Losing My Edge, and Found Self-Help That Actually Works—A True Story*, by Dan Harris
- *On the Shortness of Life*, by Seneca
- *Crush It! Why NOW Is the Time to Cash in on Your Passion*, by Gary Vaynerchuk
- *#AskGaryVee: One Entrepreneur's Take on Leadership, Social Media, and Self-Awareness*, by Gary Vaynerchuk
- *The Power of Now: A Guide to Spiritual Enlightenment*, by Eckhart Tolle
- *Are You Fully Charged?* by Tom Rath
- *A Short Guide to a Happy Life*, by Anna Quindlen
- *The 10X Rule*, by Grant Cardone
- *Born Standing Up*, by Steve Martin
- *What Got You Here Won't Get You There*, by Marshall Goldsmith
- *The Art of Possibility*, by Rosamund Stone Zander and Benjamin Zander
- *Practical Intuition*, by Laura Day
- *Start with Why*, by Simon Sinek
- *A Return to Love*, by Marianne Williamson
- *Think and Grow Rich*, by Napoleon Hill
- *The Last Lecture*, by Randy Pausch

- *Secrets of the Millionaire Mind*, by T. Harv Eker
- *Unlimited Power*, by Anthony Robbins
- *Outliers*, by Malcolm Gladwell
- *Delivering Happiness: A Path to Profits, Passion, and Purpose*, by Tony Hsieh
- *The 7 Habits of Highly Effective People*, by Stephen R. Covey
- *Mindset*, by Carol S. Dweck, PhD
- *The Daily Show (The Book): An Oral History as Told by Jon Stewart, the Correspondents, Staff, and Guests*
- *The Prophet*, by Kahlil Gibran
- *Getting Unstuck*, by Pema Chodron
- *Life without Limits: Inspiration for a Ridiculously Good Life*, by Nick Vujicic
- *The Power of Habit*, by Charles Duhigg
- *The Seven Spiritual Laws of Success*, by Deepak Chopra
- *How to Stop Worrying and Start Living*, by Dale Carnegie
- *Daring Greatly*, by Brené Brown, PhD
- *The 80/20 Principle*, by Richard Koch
- *The 4-Hour Workweek*, by Tim Ferriss
- *Tools of Titans*, by Tim Ferriss
- *Extreme Ownership: How U.S. Navy SEALs Lead and Win*, by Jocko Willink and Leif Babin
- *The School of Greatness: A Real-World Guide to Living Bigger, Loving Deeper, and Leaving a Legacy*, by Lewis Howes

QUESTIONS FOR MOTIVATION, INSPIRATION, AND DISCOVERY

When was the last time you tried something new?

Who do you sometimes compare yourself to?

What gets you excited about life?

What life lesson did you learn the hard way, and what are you doing about it today?

What do you wish you spent more time doing five years ago? Go do that.

Do you ask enough questions, or do you settle for what you know?

What can you do today that you were not capable of a year ago?

Do you think crying is a sign of weakness or strength? Why?

What would you do differently if you knew nobody would judge you?

Do you celebrate the things you do have?

If not now, then when?

If you had a friend who spoke to you in the same way that you sometimes speak to yourself, how long would you allow this person to be your friend?

If you had to teach something, what would you teach?

What would you regret not fully doing, being, or having in your life?

Are you holding on to something you need to let go of?

When you are eighty years old, what will matter to you the most?

How old would you be if you didn't know how old you are?

When it's all said and done, will you have said more than you've done?

If the average human life span was forty years, how would you live your life differently?

Which is worse: failing or never trying?

When was the last time you listened to the sound of your own breathing?

What's something you know you do differently than most people?

What is the most desirable trait another person can possess?

What are you most grateful for?

Are you more worried about doing things right or doing the right things?

Can you describe your life in a six-word sentence?

What is the most defining moment of your life thus far?

Have you ever regretted something you did not say or do?

Has your greatest fear ever come true?

What do you love most about yourself?

What small act of kindness were you once shown that you will never forget?

Do you own your things, or do your things own you?

What are your top five personal values?

What personal prisons have you built out of fear?

What one thing have you not done that you really want to do?

If you haven't achieved it yet, what do you have to lose?

What is the most important thing you could do right now in your personal life?

If happiness was the national currency, what kind of work would make you rich?

What is your number one goal for the next six months?

Are you happy with yourself?

What are three moral rules you will never break?

What does it mean to allow another person to truly love you?

If your life was a novel, what would be the title and how would your story end?

When do you feel most like yourself?

How do you know when it's time to continue holding on or time to let go?

How do you define success?

What have you read online recently that inspired you?

If you left this life tomorrow, how would you be remembered?

What do you owe yourself?

Can you think of a time when impossible became possible?

How many of your friends would you trust with your life?

What stands between you and happiness?

How do you find the strength to do what you know in your heart is right?

Where do you find peace?

How short would your life have to be before you would start living differently today?

When does silence convey more meaning than words?

How do you spend the majority of your free time?

Who do you think of first when you think of "success"? Go find that person.

How will today matter in five years from now?

Do you see to believe or believe to see?

How are you pursuing your dreams right now?

What's the next big step you need to take?

What has been the most terrifying moment of your life thus far? Good news: you're still here.

If you could take a single photograph of your life, what would it look like?

Is the reward worth the risk?

What are the primary components of a happy life?

What is your favorite song and why?

With the resources you have right now, what can you do to bring yourself closer to your goal?

What is the nicest thing someone has ever done for you? And why did you let them?

What makes you angry? Why? What can you do about it today?

If you could go back in time and tell a younger version of yourself one thing, what would you say? Follow that advice today.

What do you do to deliberately impress others? Stop doing it.

What book has had the greatest influence on your life? It may be time to reread it.

What three questions do you wish you knew the answers to? Start looking for them.

What is the greatest peer pressure you've ever felt, and how did you overcome it?

What's been on your mind most lately? What's one action you can take today to close that gap?

What chances do you wish you had taken? Your heart's still beating; you still have time.

What motivates you to go to work each day?

What is your greatest strength and your greatest weakness? List them out and post them in three places.

What motivates you to be your best? Cultivate more of that.

When you look into the past, what do you miss the most? How can you bring that back to your present day?

What is the most spontaneous thing you've ever done? Is it time to do it again?

What makes you uncomfortable? Consider moving closer to that.

What life lessons did you have to experience firsthand before you fully understood them?

What's the best part of being you?

How many people do you love? Let them know today. Don't wait.

What's the best decision you've ever made and why? How could you repeat that process today?

What was your last major accomplishment? Did you celebrate it? If not, go do that. If you did, take a few minutes, close your eyes, and remember what that felt like.

Through all of life's twists and turns, who has been there for you? Go thank them today.

Who is your mentor, and what have you learned from them? Let them know.

What do you think about when you lie awake in bed?

What's something most people don't know about you and why not?

If you could relive yesterday, what would you do differently?

What do you do over and over again that you hate doing?

Now that you know, what do you get out of this type of behavior?

What do you understand today about your life that you did not understand a year ago?

Whose life have you had the greatest impact on and why?

How would you spend your ideal day? Go make those plans and make it happen soon.

What is the best advice you have ever received? And why? Did you thank that person? If not, go do that.

What positive changes have you made in your life recently? Have you shared those accomplishments with anyone? If so, great. If not, go do that.

Who makes you feel good about yourself? Awesome, spend more time with people like that.

What type of person angers you the most? Do you see any of your own bad habits in that person's behavior?

What is your most striking physical attribute?

What has fear of failure stopped you from doing?

Whom would you like to forgive? Are you ready to take action? If not now, when?

What do you want more of in your life?

What do you want less of in your life?

Who depends on you?

Other than money, what else have you gained from your current job?

What do you sometimes pretend you understand that you really don't?

What music do you listen to to lift your spirits when you're feeling down? Have it ready to go at all times.

How much money per month is enough for you to live comfortably?

What is your favorite place on Earth? When was the last time you were there? Maybe it's time to go there.

What is the most recent dream you remember having while sleeping?

When did you not speak up when you should have?

What have you lost interest in recently? Are you still doing it? If so, why?

Have you achieved your life's goals? If not yet, what are the things that you're currently doing to achieve those goals?

Are you affected by others' opinions about you? Do they influence how you lead your life?

What are you passionate about? Are you doing anything to pursue it?

Are you willing to try a new adventure? What would it be?

What was your childhood dream? Have you achieved it?

How can you make your community a better place?

When you look in a mirror, what do you see?

What do you like to tell yourself whenever you're down or disappointed?

Where is your "happy place"? Can you stay there most of the time?

What are the three most important aspects of your life right now? What are you doing to protect and cultivate them?

What material things can you live without? Consider donating them to someone in need or less fortunate.

What natural phenomenon fascinates you the most? Have you ever witnessed it in person? If not, consider doing that.

If you could make a difference in someone's life, who would you choose to help, and what are the things that you could do to make his/her life better?

How can you make yourself more productive every day?

Have you found your soul mate? If not yet, do you believe that he/she will still come to your life?

If you wanted to pamper yourself today, what activity would you do?

If you had the opportunity to be an entrepreneur, what would be your smart business idea?

Is there someone who you think owes you an apology? Are you ready to forgive him/her?

What legacy would you like to leave behind?

What will it take to make you get out of your comfort zone?

Have you reached your full potential, or is there still room for improvement?

Have you ever watched the sun rise or set? How did it make you feel?

If you could pack your most valuable possessions in one bag, what would the contents be?

If you could be a superhero for a day, who would you like to be and why?

If it was possible to trade your life with another person who you admire or idolize, who would you do it with and why?

What do you consider your biggest weakness? How can you overcome this?

What have you learned today?

Who can make you laugh so hard that you end up crying?

If money is not an issue, what would you be doing right now?

Name three of your biggest fears, and if they came true, how would you handle them?

Do you easily admit to your mistakes, or do you always make up excuses for your behavior?

Are you afraid of committing mistakes, or do you welcome them so you can be a stronger person?

If you could influence others to follow your lead, what important thing would you like them to do?

Do you have any exciting plans for the coming year? What are they?

If your life was a book, what would be its title?

If you were given the opportunity to start a new life and erase your past, would you take it? Why or why not?

Would you rather be a genius who has a complicated life or an average thinker who takes pleasure in simple things?

Are you the one controlling your life, or do life events control you?

What principles in life do you value the most? Do you strive to live by them?

What sacrifices are you willing to make in order to realize your dreams?

What movie made the biggest impact on you? Go watch it again.

If your partner asked you to make a sacrifice for him/her, would you grant that request? Why or why not?

If you could re-create one precious moment in your life, what would it be, and why would you choose it?

When was the last time you rewarded yourself with something special?

What good habits would you like to acquire? What are the steps you should take to have them?

Do you consider yourself a positive person? How can you have a positive attitude most of the time?

Do you devote some time and effort for your personal growth and development?

What was the most powerful emotion that you have ever felt?

Who do you love, and what are you doing about it?

For more, visit www.joshhmiller.com.

RELATIONSHIP AUDITING

Think about all the people in your life and list them out
here. Then think about what you want for your life in one,
five, and ten years. Will these people help you get there?
If not, it might be time to reconsider if they are worthy
of a spot in your life.

....

....

....

....

....

GRATITUDE JOURNAL*

Use this space to write down things that inspire you and make you happy—things you've learned, acts of kindness you committed or witnessed, or any other thing that's going to help you feel gratitude for the journey you're on every day.

*As much as I would love to have included two hundred pages for you to journal, my editor said that was overkill. Start with these pages, then go get yourself a proper journal—it will be worth it.

....

....

....

GOAL-SETTING WORKSHEET

Use this as a starting template to get thinking about your goals. If you need a refresher, go back to chapter seven and reread the section "Goal Setting."

Think of your goal. Is it:

- **S**pecific?
- **M**easurable?
- **A**chievable?
- **R**elevant?
- **T**ime-based?

If it meets all those criteria, ask yourself why it's important to you. Give three reasons.

....

....

....

There are likely things you will need to give up in service of this goal. List three things you are willing to sacrifice to make your goal happen.

....

....

....

For extra credit, go back to the "Relationship Auditing" section of the appendix (for a refresher on why this is important, head back to chapter one). Ask who you can reach out to to help you reach your goal.

Start today.

ABOUT THE AUTHOR

JOSHUA MILLER is a certified personal and executive coach who spends his life supporting people to bury their bullshit and uncover the greatness they already have. He started his career as a creative director in advertising, responsible for the campaign strategies of Fortune 100 brands, and now creates and supports executive leadership development for many of the same companies. He's a Ted Talk speaker, a LinkedIn Top Influencer, a contributing writer for Thrive Global and Medium, and the creator of "MyInstantCoach," the first life-coaching app for the iPhone. Married with two children and living in California, this former Manhattanite is currently dedicating himself to finding the best "slice" on the West Coast.

Made in the USA
San Bernardino, CA
05 June 2018